MAKE MORE WORK LESS by CONNECTING

Releasing the Power of
Effective Communication

Make More Work Less by Connecting
Releasing the Power of Effective Communication

Published by
10-10-10 Publishing
Ontario, Canada

Copyright © FEB 2020
by Fong Chua and Jessica Ng
Edmonton, Alberta, Canada
www.makemoreworklessbook.com/connect

All Rights Reserved. No part of this book may be reproduced in any form, by photocopying or by electronic or mechanical means, including information storage or retrieval systems, without permission in writing from both the copyright owner and the publisher of this book. The opinions and conclusions drawn in this book are solely those of the author. The author and the publisher bear no liability in connection with the use of the ideas presented.

For information about special discounts for bulk purchases, please contact the Assurance Real Estate Acquisitions Inc.

Printed in the United States of America

ISBN: 978-1-77277-330-9 (paperback)
ISBN: 978-1-77277-331-6 (e-book)

First Edition

MAKE MORE WORK LESS by CONNECTING

Releasing the Power of Effective Communication

Fong Chua & Jessica Ng

Featuring Advisors:
Gloria Bosma, Dr. Ganz Ferrance,
Shin Kawaguchi, Chan Kawaguchi,
Stacy Richter, and Glenda Sheard

- ABOUT THE AUTHORS -

Assurance Real Estate Acquisitions Inc. was brought together by the managing partners, Jessica Ng and Fong Chua, to bring to life their beliefs in adding value to people. This partnership specializes in uniting the right people, the right project and the right solution, all while adding value to all those involved, creating a win-win environment. Assurance Real Estate Acquisitions Inc. places great emphasis on relational capital, which is why we treat our clients and partners the same as our loved ones.

Starting out as engineers and winners of the Deal Makers Award in real estate, Fong and Jessica have the technical skills and attention to details to ensure that all projects are of value for all parties involved. We have many insider relationships with investors and agents, which allows us to have access to great deals first. Since then, Fong and Jessica have become coaches, entrepreneurs, and speakers. Our philosophy is simple, we enjoy working with individuals who seek to grow, and assist them in unlocking their potential to become champions. When it comes to clients, three words describe our focus: loyalty, relationships, and results. Therefore, we believe that clients should be for life and why we treat our client's visions and aspirations like they were our own.

Our Mission: To bring wealth, be it financial, knowledge or security, to all those who seek it. With our expertise and heart, it is our mission to impact as many people as we can by showing them how they can achieve more than they think.

This book is dedicated to:

Our clients and partners who showed us that there are many people who could use our guidance, and that by sharing our knowledge, will lead them and us to greater success. To our parents for their great lessons in life: ethics and the meaning of hard work. Without these characteristics, we would not have had the foundation that got us to where we are today.

Our advisors, Gloria Bosma, Dr. Ganz Ferrance, Chan Kawaguchi, Shin Kawaguchi, Stacy Richter, and Glenda Sheard who encourage, support and challenge us. We wouldn't be where we are today if it weren't for them.

Without the support and dedication that we committed to our business and to each other, our ventures would not be possible.

- ACKNOWLEDGEMENTS -

We would like to acknowledge and thank all those involved with the publishing of this book for their hard work and care in putting this book together. We are absolutely thankful for their patience and time spent dealing with our requests.

Thank you to everyone that supported us in this venture: from writing (Gloria Bosma, Dr. Ganz Ferrance, Chan Kawaguchi, Shin Kawaguchi, Stacy Richter, and Glenda Sheard), to editing (Louise Harris, LAST Research & Editing), to cover design (Jong Chua, Just Creative Inc.), to photography (Krzysztof Wisniewski, The PhotoMotion), to our coaches' (Derek Eurales, Paul Xavier, and the World's #1 Wealth Coach JT Foxx) for their guidance and assistance. Your assistance, support and motivation are deeply appreciated. We would also like to extend a heartfelt thank you to our circle of loving family, friends, clients and peers who have all been very supportive and encouraging to us.

Finally, we cannot thank Reggie Batts enough for his friendship and phenomenal support during this venture. Thank you, Reggie for your belief in us and for writing the foreword to this book. We would not be where we are if not for you.

- CONTENTS -

- FOREWORD - 2

- INTRODUCTION - 6

Chapter - 1 -
Connect Through Thought 10

Chapter - 2 -
Connect Through Desire 26

Chapter - 3 -
Connect Through Emotions..40

Chapter - 4 -
Connect Through Senses...56

Chapter - 5 -
Teaching Connects..80

Chapter - 6 -
Community Connects..96

Chapter - 7 -
Relationships Connects 110

Chapter - 8 -
Sales/Marketing Connects..122

Chapter - 9 -
Investing Connects..134

Chapter - 10 -
Entrepreneurship Connects..146

Chapter - 11 -
Coaching Connects...158

Chapter - 12 -
Connect Through Stories 182

PUBLIC SPEAKING TIPS 202

- FINAL THOUGHTS -..204

About Gloria Bosma 206
About Ganz Ferrance 208
About Chan Kawaguchi 210
About Shin Kawaguchi 212
About Stacy Richter 214
About Glenda Sheard 216

Additional Content 218

Recommended Resource List 220

MAKE MORE WORK LESS by CONNECTING

- FOREWORD -

I have witnessed great changes in both Jessica and Fong since I first met them. Having worked and known them for the past 10 years, I have seen them go from left-brained introverts to a tag team who is impacting everyone they meet. Through coaching, taking-action, and building relationships, they have achieved numerous goals and successes that many would never attempt. I have always stressed that "If you are not growing then you are dying", and when it comes to Jessica and Fong, they have taken the teachings of building strong strategic relationships, entrepreneurship, and mindset to the next level into their personal lives and businesses, strived, and grew.

Make More Work Less by Connecting is put together to help you understand the importance of effective communication, to help you achieve more happiness and success, and at the same time, *Make More and Work Less*. Not only do they unlock the techniques to effective communication like audience engagement, emotion and structure, Jessica and Fong have compiled here a series of experts to illustrate to you how important effective communication is in all areas of our lives. I have witnessed their growth throughout the years and have seen them applying these techniques in their conversations, business, and on-stage presentations first-hand. By following the techniques outlined in *Make More Work Less by Connecting* you too can start spreading your message to more people, save time, and *Make More and Work Less*.

Jessica and Fong have truly understood the value of effective communication, and, in doing so, have developed friendships

MAKE MORE WORK LESS by CONNECTING

with individuals all over the world. From members of my team to myself (an international speaker), when the names Jessica and Fong are mentioned, we know we are dealing with people who are caring, loyal, and full of integrity. As you go through the pages of *Make More Work Less by Connecting* you will see yourself, why Jessica and Fong have been able to build long-lasting strategic relationships, succeeded in entrepreneurship and have great stage presences. It will motivate you to step out of your comfort zone and challenge yourself by changing your mindset and surrounding yourself with a support group that will unlock brand new opportunities and adventures that you have never even dreamed of. With just a few simple strategies, you too will have the skills to communicate and connect effectively that will propel you to *Make More and Work Less*.

The strategies demonstrated within the pages of this book by Jessica and Fong along with their own advisors will unlock secrets and opportunities that will guide you to get your message out to more people and build strong relationships along the way.

In this book:

- You will learn from experts, their strategies and techniques that will help you connect with your audience, clients, co-workers, and your family.

- You will find tips to creating effective speeches and craft stories that will have your message heard.

Soon, you will discover that communication affects all aspects of our lives and that if you want to have the best results in whatever it is you do, then being an effective

MAKE MORE WORK LESS by CONNECTING

communicator will allow you to achieve the success that you always wanted. There is not enough time in the day for you to connect with everyone, therefore the more effective you are in connecting with more people the more you will achieve.

Now is the time to unleash the power of effective communication, and connect with the individuals, communities, and clients in your world and see how easy it is to unlock your potential to live and work on your own terms!

Reggie Batts

World-renowned International Speaker and Best-selling Author of *Mindset for Success.*

MAKE MORE WORK LESS by CONNECTING

MAKE MORE WORK LESS by CONNECTING

- INTRODUCTION -

Fong and I had just gone to our first real estate event. We were excited to attend the three-day event to learn what we needed to start our path to financial freedom via real estate. We dreamt about how we would no longer have to worry about losing our engineering jobs should the oil and gas industry plummet; about how we can help out our families, especially the ones overseas or those who aren't as well off; and how we can finally make a bigger and better impact on our community. Things will be great!

Fast forward to the three-day course. We had learned so much, yet we realized there was still so much we needed to know to get us to where we wanted to be. We had no idea that there was so much to real estate. We needed more education to get where we wanted to go. To help our families, friends, and community and to live life on our own terms, not what our bosses tell us to do. We were scared out of our minds. We had just signed up for what we felt was a HUGE cost to learn the advanced techniques of real estate investing. It didn't matter though, our dreams and desires told us it was the right thing to do.

As we continued to learn about real estate and a lot of other investment and business strategies over the years, we have reached a level where we are building a great financial empire with real estate, investments and other businesses. Looking back, we were SHOCKED to see how much time and money we were spending on courses, books, and speaking. We found that becoming an effective communicator was one major component as to how we are able to get to where we are today. Without being able to

MAKE MORE WORK LESS by CONNECTING

communicate effectively and connect with people, we would not have been able to build a team of professionals, partners, and clients to get us to where we want to be, to be able to *Make More* and *Work Less*.

We realize that to become an effective communicator is a very personal and delicate process that requires a personal touch and assessment. Through this book, we will share with you, elements of an effective communicator, how to become an effective communicator, and how to use communication to add value to others and achieve your goals. We hope that this will give you a chance to see for yourself how important effective communication is in any aspect of your life.

We have also been very fortunate to have a few of our partners, coaches, and advisors from all different industries and expertise, here with us. They will share with you their secrets and experiences in becoming effective communicators allowing them to connect at a deeper level.

Although this is but an introduction to the importance of becoming an effective communicator, we hope that it will open your minds to explore the art of communicating. By applying the communication skills that you learn to your everyday life, it will lead you to deeper connections, success, and allow you to *Make More and Work Less*.

We sincerely hope to help you achieve your dreams without having to spend the same amount of time and money that we have spent. It is our hope also that you will use your new-found skills to help your community and those in it. As Napoleon Hill put it, "*It is literally true that you can succeed best and quickest by helping others succeed*".

MAKE MORE WORK LESS by CONNECTING

Now, let's get into the keys of the book!

Thank you and enjoy!

MAKE MORE WORK LESS by CONNECTING

Chapter - 1 -
Connect Through Thought

MAKE MORE WORK LESS by CONNECTING

MAKE MORE WORK LESS by CONNECTING

"What would you recommend my child to take in school?", "What would you say is the most important skill set one must have to succeed?", "If you had a chance to go back in time, what one thing do you wish you would have focused on more?" We have been asked these questions a lot by clients, audience members, partners, family, friends, and sometimes by random strangers after a cup of coffee. To each of these questions, we have one answer -- **Speaking Effectively**. Developing strong effective communication skills is probably the one thing that ties everything that you want all together. Imagine having the most impressive resume one can put together, but you are constantly stuttering in the interview. Or having the best ideas for increasing your company's revenues, but you are constantly staring at the ground while presenting it to your supervisor. If one wants to grow, advance in a company, build relationships, network, and *Make More and Work Less*, one must be an effective communicator. Once you communicate effectively then you will connect with the person or persons who are communicating with you. It is very common that the next words that we hear are: "*Well, I can't speak so what else do you recommend?*" or "*Some people are just gifted with that skill, I can't do it.*" To that we reply, "*Then you are right...you can't.*"

Mind Set

Everything that happens, happens because of a thought. As Henry Ford once said, "*Whether you think you can, or you think you can't, you're right.*" If you don't ever think you can speak effectively, then you will never take the action to learn how to speak effectively. You may or may not become a professional speaker making $50,000 for an hour to talk, but you will definitely be a much more effective speaker than you

MAKE MORE WORK LESS by CONNECTING

are now. The mind is a very fragile thing, if you feed it with negative thoughts, you will see more negative things. Conversely, if you tell yourself that your day will be great, then, you will go on with your day looking subconsciously for all the great things that day. For instance, Do Not Sing "It's a Small World" ...Who is singing it right now? Who will be humming it throughout the day? That's right -- all of you. Even if I specifically told you NOT to sing it, the thought of the song appears and remains. Put it in your mind that you CAN be an effective communicator and an effective speaker. Don't worry about the how. We will get to that later in the book. Right now, just picture yourself as an effective speaker.

Imagine yourself speaking with confidence, your audience is attentive, and they are nodding with approval. You know you have connected with them; you know that your thoughts, ideas, and message has gotten across to them. You feel great! Now hold that thought. How does one hold that thought? How do you maintain that mentality so that with any adversity, one does not give up? Well, if you want to succeed at anything, or, in this case, to be an effective communicator, remember the acronym: CAP

C: Confidence
A: Attitude
P: Persistence

Let's explore these a little more closely now.

MAKE MORE WORK LESS by CONNECTING

Confidence

Sometimes, confidence trips us all. We find out the skills we are lacking and put in an effort to learning them, but then we start doubting ourselves. Can I really do this? What if I forget something? What if I don't know enough?

As with everything, you build confidence by doing it. You learn the skills, practice it and apply it. To help you understand how we build confidence, we will explain the four levels that we all go through when developing confidence. The first level is unconscious incompetence, the second is conscious incompetence, the third level is conscious competence, and the last level is unconscious competence.

1 – Unconscious Incompetence
2 – Conscious Incompetence
3 – Conscious Competence
4 – Unconscious Competence

Let's use speaking effectively as an example. There are some people who didn't know there is such thing as "speaking effectively" they just talk and say words – *Level 1 – They don't know what they don't know.*

Later they watch a debate on TV, or meet people and converse and said to themselves "*Wow. Something they said really struck me. They are really good at expressing their ideas! I wish I can do that.*" – *Level 2 – They know what they don't know.*

After wishing that they can speak better, they searched for speaking classes like Dale Carnegie, Toastmasters, or seek

MAKE MORE WORK LESS by CONNECTING

a speaking coach and started to learn how to speak more effectively – *Level 3 – They know.*

After doing speeches, networking more, and doing more presentations, speaking effectively becomes easier and a part of them – *Level 4 – They KNOW it naturally.*

Once you are competent, you need to stop doubting yourself and simply trust that you are able to do it. You didn't give up on reading just because you weren't sure of yourself, did you? We hope you had just kept practicing until you were more comfortable. Anything you do in life is like that. Just as you trust that you can read, you should trust in your abilities to learn the skills to speak effectively and apply it.

Attitude

Even if we were confident, we will need more than just that to help our mindset. We must have a good attitude. You might be asking yourself, how do I get that? The key is in your thoughts. The more you think that you can become an effective speaker, the easier it will get. It is all in your attitude and how you think about opportunities presented to you.

Why is speaking effectively important? Why must one connect with people on a daily basis? As you know by now, connecting with people is the key to getting your message across. The reason why we say anything or do anything, is because we have something to offer, or there is something that we want to acquire. When you suggest to your spouse that you want to go to a specific restaurant, you are presenting an idea that you want your spouse to '*buy*' into. When you go into an interview you want to '*sell*' yourself well enough to the interviewer that they will '*buy*' you. If one does

MAKE MORE WORK LESS by CONNECTING

not speak effectively to the audience, then their idea, suggestion, or message will not be bought. Therefore, when given the opportunity, one must have the right and positive attitude that one can speak effectively and connect with the person or persons you are conversing with.

Before we continue, we want to tell you a little story:

> *The first time I was told to speak on stage, I was terrified. I was thinking: "I can't do this! Two hours? What will I talk about? What if the audience is bored? These people paid good money for this event, is what I have to share of value to them? On and on, I went destroying my self-esteem and confidence. Doubting myself nonstop.*
>
> *It wasn't until my coach put the situation into perspective for me that my attitude changed. Two hours is nothing more than 12, 10-minute topics. 12 topics is easy to develop. How can I deliver my topics in a way that is exciting and interesting? As long as one person picks up something from my speech, I have made a difference.*

When you read the two scenarios, did you feel the difference as to how your mind started to think differently? By asking different questions your mind will start feeling positively and hopeful.

The fact is that we all have the ability to change our attitude about any situation. We may require some help by others, or some practice within ourselves. As long as we keep reminding ourselves as to "Why" what we are doing is important and knowing that our attitude is everything, then we will start adjusting our attitude to suit the situation for us to succeed. By doing so, we could possibly see a hidden opportunity when most people would see an obstacle.

Persistence

When you were young, do you remember learning to walk? Even if you don't, you know what the process is right? As a child, you started crawling. Then you would stand with some support, and as your legs grew stronger, you were able to stand without support. Finally, you would try to walk. Chances are high that the first few times you tried to walk, you stumbled and fell. Maybe you cried, maybe you didn't. Either way, you would try again and again to walk. Your parents or guardians would encourage you to do it.

Sometimes, you might just want to give up, but with so many people cheering you on, you would try again and again. Finally, with enough practice and persistence, you unlocked the keys to walking. Now, walking is so second nature to you that you don't even have to tell yourself, *"put your left foot out, step down, transfer your weight over to the left foot and bring your right foot forward."* No, you can now walk without thinking.

Now that we are older, we won't necessarily have such a large fan base cheering us on to walk. This is why our attitude and our confidence are so important. Even so, there are times when we just want to give up. Things have gotten hard and things might not be going well. This is why we need persistence.

A key point we want to unlock at this point is what we call your "Why." Why are you working on this goal? Why is this so important to you? Why keep working on it when it's so hard? Why, why, why. This is what will keep pushing you on when things are getting you down and your attitude and confidence in yourself are no longer enough. If your why doesn't make you cry, keep working on finding it.

Your why becomes your mission and is the foundation of what you are building. If your foundation is weak, then what you are building will crumble in a matter of time. If your foundation is strong, no matter what wind or hardship is blowing on you, you hold the key to rebuilding because your foundation is still there.

To start having a good mindset that looks for opportunity rather than obstacles, remember the acronym CAP:

Confidence, Attitude, and Persistence.

Always believe in yourself, think positively about yourself and most of all: Trust in your mission.

You might now be thinking, sure I can do those things, but how? To help aid you in that, we present two ideas: Vision Boards and Mind Feeding.

Vision Board

Vision board is a presentation with pictures and words on it to help you visualize your goals. It should be placed some place visible to you daily as a reminder for yourself. Because you have picked up this book, we will assume that part of your goal is to connect with people via effective communication. However, that is not the only thing in which vision boards are all about. Remember how we talked about

MAKE MORE WORK LESS by CONNECTING

your why? Your vision board should have that too. When times are hard, look at your vision board to give yourself the strength to continue.

Each vision board is unique to the person. Some categories may not apply to you while other categories might not apply to others. Feel free to explore the possibilities of your vision board and to make it something you believe in yourself.

The more you see it, the more your mind will be "*looking*" for opportunities that bring those items to you. Instead of thinking that the items are dreams or farfetched goals, your mind will slowly believe that you already are in possession of the items in your vision board.

A great story about a powerful vision is that of an individual on the Internet. We highly recommend that you read through the full story. Simply search *"How a Password Changed my Life" – by Mauricio Estrella*. Mauricio basically used his computer password that requires monthly changing as a creative reminder of what he wanted in his life. Needing to access his computer multiple times a day, the vision of his password is triggered multiple times a day. Here are a few examples of the passwords that he used:

Quit@smoking4ever
Save4trip@thailand
No@drinking2months
Get@c4t!
Save4@ring

What an incredible idea. Maybe your next password will be:
#1!$p3@k3r

Mind Feed

Mind feed means feeding your brain with positive and stimulating things. Instead of watching TV and listening to the radio, consider reading or listening to a business book. There are many books and audio books out there that can uplift our spirit and remind us of our why. There are also many books, audio books, and podcasts out there that can enhance or teach us new skills. What do you let in your mind?

Ever hear people say: *"Boy! Am I having a bad day..."* or *"Gee, nothing seems to be going my way today."* Those things are happening all the time but never seemed to bother them before that day. The moment a person deems something is negative, awful, or bad luck; their brains now are attracting everything else that can be interpreted as bad luck. They have concluded at the beginning of the day that they are having a bad day. Hence, mentally, they are looking for all the negative things happening around them to fulfill the notion of a bad day. It is this aspect that makes mind feeding important. If you feed your mind with inspiration, motivation, and information that will enrich your mind then you will live each and every day feeling inspired, motivated, and attracting the feelings and opportunities you are feeding your mind. At a minimum, we should all be feeding our minds every day for 30 minutes to an hour first thing in the morning. What better way to start the day than feeding your mind with riches?

Everything makes a difference. What does your alarm clock sound like? Is it loud and annoying? You cannot wait to turn it off, right? How do you feel when it goes off and you end it? Do you feel great or annoyed? Is that really how you want to start the day? Alarms in general signify something negative.

MAKE MORE WORK LESS by CONNECTING

Fire alarm, burglar alarm, emergency alarm -- all signifying something bad is about to happen, so why not start seeing your alarm clock as an opportunity clock. Each time it sounds, it signifies that great things are in store for you! To add to that thought, why not change the annoying sound of the alarm or "opportunity" to be your favorite uplifting song? Personally, my opportunity clock plays "*You've got the Touch*" by Stan Bush every morning. I must say I wake up to the feeling of having the POWER to do anything!

Most people think garbage in means garbage out. Nido Qubein told us otherwise. He told us that when garbage gets in your mind, it doesn't just stay. It gets pregnant and gives birth to triplets! So be careful what you let in your mind. Be selective about it and ensure that it supports the goals you have set for yourself on your vision board.

Masterminds

The saying goes, "Who you spend time with is who you will become." If you want to be successful, spend time with successful people and do what they do. If you want to speak effectively, spend time with effective speakers and others who also want to become effective speakers. Mastermind groups are groups where like-minded people get together to support and assist each other with their goals. They will bounce ideas with each other, discuss what works and what doesn't. The group also acts as everyone's accountability partners, making sure that everyone's goals are met or are heading in the right direction. There are many different mastermind groups out there for you to choose. Similarly, organizations like Toastmasters International and Dale Carnegie can provide you with a stepping stone environment that will assist you in becoming an effective speaker.

MAKE MORE WORK LESS by CONNECTING

Mindset is a very important part to our road to success and in itself can be a very large topic. Two great books on mindset that we highly recommend are *Change your Mind Change your Results – #1 Proven Success Strategies* by Shawn Shewchuk and *Mindset for Success: Developing and maintaining the mindset to succeed in life & business* – by Reggie Batts. We had the privilege of working with Mr. Shewchuk and Mr. Batts, and can say without a doubt that their books and their teachings have changed our mindsets to seek opportunities, results, and success. Feel free to contact us for more information.

A list of good books and audiobooks for mind feeding has been included at the end of this book as a reference for you.

If you can speak effectively and connect, wouldn't you say you would have a better chance at that job? Wouldn't you think that you would be able to land that client? Wouldn't you think that you will be able to sell more? Wouldn't that make things a whole lot easier allowing you to *Make More and Work Less*?

Throughout the rest of this book you will discover the backbone of effective communication, how to connect with whom you are speaking, how to engage emotionally, learn techniques and skills for an impactful presentation and much more. You will also be introduced to experts in their fields who will share with you their experiences and secrets as to how they utilized effective communication skills to connect, get to where they are today, and to reach utmost levels of success: Teacher – Gloria Bosma, Relationship Expert – Dr. Ganz Ferrance, Sales and Marketing Mastermind – Stacy Richter, Entrepreneur Disruptor – Chan Kawaguchi, Investment

MAKE MORE WORK LESS by CONNECTING

Expert – Shin Kawaguchi, and Donation Specialist – Glenda Sheard.

MAKE MORE WORK LESS by CONNECTING

Chapter 1 – Connect Through Thought

"We have two ears and one mouth so that we can listen twice as much as we speak."

- Epictetus -

Assurance Keys to Connecting

- Mindset – Believe you are an effective communicator.

- Confidence
    - You don't know what you don't know
    - You know what you don't know
    - You know
    - You know it naturally

- Attitude
    - Positive attitude leads to positive results.

- Persistence
    - Keep at it.

- Mind Feed
    - Opportunity Clock

- Vision Boards

- Masterminds
    - Who you spend time with is who you will become.

MAKE MORE WORK LESS by CONNECTING

Chapter - 2 -
Connect Through Desire

MAKE MORE WORK LESS by CONNECTING

Connecting Vs Communicating

Have you ever wondered, did that person even hear what I said? Or understand what I wanted? Or even care about what you requested? How many of you have experienced someone walking towards you and ask, "*How are you doing?*" and before you even have a chance to answer, he or she has already walked past you? What our society is not doing well now is connecting. We communicate, but we are not connecting. The absolute opposite results are achieved. You might be thinking now, "*Isn't plain communication the same thing as connecting?*" We understand why you might think that just talking to someone is connecting with someone. Let's look at the following example:

> Who here has ever called an energy provider to sort out billing problems? I wanted to pay my bill using a different account. I called once and realized that there is no menu option to speak to a person. Therefore, I had to keep selecting until I stumbled across a sub menu option for a person or kept pressing 0 repeatedly until the system gets confused and sends me to a representative. After reaching a person and explaining the situation, I was told that it was my bank's issue, even though it was not and that they will issue me a '**ticket**' to escalate the issue. I went to my bank and sure enough it was not the bank's issue. I called the energy company again, 00000000 and again explained the situation to another person who then told me that I had to resubmit the preauthorized payment form with the correct account. After being asked why they couldn't just switch it back because they already have my original authorization, they told me that they could not do so, that it was outside of

MAKE MORE WORK LESS by CONNECTING

their abilities and that they will issue me a '**ticket**' and escalate the issue. Nothing happened. Funds were still withdrawn from the wrong account, e-mails have been sent and '**tickets**' were issued. No follow up calls from the energy company and no results. I called again, 000000 and was asked again what they can do for me, knowing that this first gate keeper is not authorized to do anything, I asked specifically for a supervisor. After a long discussion as to why I wanted a supervisor in which I told them it's not them but the system, they assured me that they will issue me a '**TICKET**' to escalate the issue, in which I said: "NO MORE TICKETS. They don't go anywhere!" I finally got put through to a supervisor. Before the supervisor even spoke, I told him that I do not want any 'tickets' to be issued. In which he replied: "what seems to be the problem?" I explained the situation with the history of the interactions. He then told me that he will fix the issue and get everything resolved. I said thank you in which he said "Not a problem. Sorry for what you had to go through. If you can please fill out the preauthorized form and send it back, we will issue a ticket to escalate the issue". I ended the call.

Now, I will ask you: "*Was communication being done?*" – Yes. "*Was there a connection?*" – No. The person working for the energy company was communicating with a script. He did not connect with the client and did not listen to what the client wanted. Instead of providing customer service, he is providing a negative experience.

Listening to the customers/guests/client is the most important aspects to allow the provider to connect with them. Without connecting, they are merely just following a script without

MAKE MORE WORK LESS by CONNECTING

thinking what would make sense. What does the customer/guest or even the audience actually want? Sure, scripts and checklists are great for training and helping those who start a new job, but people must realize that scripts are just a guideline to follow and should create their own style and modify where needed.

> AT&T had a rule for all their customer service representatives requiring them to end each call with "Thank you for using AT&T." Knowing this rule, Nido, A great entrepreneur replies "No, thank you for great customer service!" In which the AT&T rep pauses and says "No, Thank YOU for using AT&T." fulfilling the requirement that they MUST end each call by saying that. Thinking that it would be fun, Nido continues to say "No. No thank YOU for your fast-reliable service." AT&T rep "um No, thank you for using AT&T." Nido "no no THANK YOU for taking care of my needs"..."THANK YOU FOR USING AT&T" click.....

What should have been a great interaction and customer service ends with the company representative rudely slamming the phone on the customer after yelling in their ear! If they would listen and connect, they would know that they could deviate from the script and be respectable.

These scenarios happen all the time. If you start to pay more attention to the words that are being said, you will soon realize that a lot of those in customer service are really going by the script and not spending the time connecting with the customer. Who here has ever gone to a drive through restaurant to be confused because you said yes to paying an extra 25 cents for unlimited refills? Or going to the counter to order just an ice cream cone to come back with more

MAKE MORE WORK LESS by CONNECTING

because you were asked if you wanted fries with that followed by "do you want that supersized?!" You can call it up selling or good old sales. But is that really what the customer wants? Because if you think about it, you can't refill a drink if you are at a drive-through area and why on earth would you want supersized fries with your ice cream cone? Get me a burger and a Coke while you are at it! Now I have a melting ice cream cone because I have to eat all that food before the ice cream!

When it comes to customer service, we are able to critique and pick out the areas where the communication is off and the connection is missing. We must do the same when we are speaking with others, either in a networking scenario, in an interview, during a keynote, during a sales presentation, through the radio, in asking for donations or in helping others. Connecting with the audience will allow you to communicate effectively.

How to Count Vs What Counts

Nido Qubein, one of the top businessmen in the world shared his thoughts about the difference between connecting and communicating. It all stems from our society focusing too much on training instead of educating. Our education system now is training the younger generation to become clerks, service people, business people, engineers, doctors, and lawyers. Our work places are putting employees into training programs to train cashiers and sale clerks, and customer service people. What businesses and our education systems are not doing enough of is 'Educating'. When we 'Train' we show you the HOW, but when we 'Educate', we show you the WHY. Training is transactional and technical while education is transformational and stays with you forever when the training is long forgotten. Nido stresses that he is not saying that training is not needed because it is required that training is provided if you want someone to do what you want them to do, but training alone cannot stand. By educating we learn how to BE while with training, we learn what to do. In school, we are trained how to count. From our parents we are taught "*what counts*". We must learn to speak and listen, observe and write. Not just hear, talk, see and scribble. By doing so, we will connect and when we connect, something happens – heart to heart, soul to soul, and mission to mission with another human being.

Six Steps to Desire

What counts in your life? What counts in their lives? This is very similar to your Why and in turn their Why. Why should the person you are talking to spend their time listening to you? Why should they build a relationship with you? Why should they care about your message? Your goal is to find their desire. That desire will come from their Why and what matters to them most.

There are a few steps that one must go through to reach desire. When you are able to communicate effectively you will be able to walk them through step by step with your questions, your actions and your information. You will find out what their Why is. Their Why will lead to a goal. Their goal will then be realized with awareness. You will then supply knowledge that fills that awareness. That knowledge will pique their interest more. Finally, with the added interest, it becomes desire.

Why→ Goal→ Awareness→ Knowledge→ Interest→ Desire

MAKE MORE WORK LESS by CONNECTING

Why
- Why are they doing what they are doing?
- What is the driving force of their actions?
- Why is it something that they are emotionally attached to?

Goal
- *Align goals with their Why*
- *Goals that when achieved will strengthen their Why*
- *Goals that excites them…making them feel more alive*

Awareness
- *Attract the attention of your audience*
- *Supply a vision that their goals can be a reality*
- *Show them what they didn't know*

Knowledge
- *Explain to them what they didn't know*
- *Give background to the information*
- *Show how the knowledge is applied and relevant*

Interest
- *Focus on the benefits and advantages*
- *Illustrate the cause and effects*
- *Contrast 'what if' scenarios*

Desire
- *Demonstrate how your information will satisfy their needs*
- *Relate back to their goals and their Why*
- *Enhance the vision of achieving their goals*

Let's look at a potential desire to become an effective communicator if we were a business entrepreneur:

MAKE MORE WORK LESS by CONNECTING

Why – To be able to spend more quality time with loved ones.

Goal – To present ideas and build relationships effectively.

Awareness – This can be done by learning to communicate effectively.

Knowledge – Communicating effectively consists of using effective language, body gestures, becoming a great storyteller, understanding your audience, and harnessing your passion.

Interest – By communicating effectively you will build better relationships, save time when networking, save effort in presenting your ideas effectively, becoming a better leader. In turn, your skills will bring in more business, train better employees, and ultimately allow you to spend more time with family as your business becomes self-running.

Desire – The sooner you develop better communication skills the sooner you can present ideas effectively, and the sooner your goals will be achieved to match your Why.

Let's look at a potential desire to become an effective communicator if we were an individual looking for a job:

Why – To be able to provide for a family of my own.

Goal – To present myself in interviews effectively.

MAKE MORE WORK LESS by CONNECTING

Awareness – *This can be done by learning to communicate effectively.*

Knowledge – *Communicating effectively consists of using effective language, body gestures, becoming a great storyteller, understanding the company you are applying for, and harnessing your passion for the role.*

Interest – *By communicating effectively you will leave a lasting impression on the interviewer, setting yourself apart from other applicants.*

Desire – *The sooner you develop better communication skills the sooner you can present yourself effectively, and the sooner you can impress an interviewer and land a job that can potentially set you up for a career*

This process will be done by you with your audience or with anyone you are connecting with.

What is in it for me?

One way of enhancing the desire is always asking "*What is in it for me?*" From your audience's point of view, the answer to that question will always be VALUE. As long as you are constantly thinking about what value you can provide your audience, then there will always be something that is "in it" for him or her. Whether it is information that you have, knowledge, contacts, a product, services etc. if you are able to position your assets as value to your counterpart, then they will be engaged.

MAKE MORE WORK LESS by CONNECTING

Once you are adding a lot of value to other people, they will, in turn, add value to you. We generally feel that if we get something from someone we must, in turn, provide something of equal value or greater to that person. When all parties are involved with adding value to each other better connections are made, stronger relationships are formed, and individuals are listening more intently.

Is this Sales?

Short answer is yes. This is sales. The reality is that we are selling all the time. The ultimate result of effective communication and connecting is really to allow you to "sell" yourself better and effectively. Whether it is for an interview, a networking event or a full sales event, your purpose is to leave a lasting impression to get a call back for a job, to book another get together with someone at a networking event, to sell a product, or to get an answer. In all four scenarios, you are selling yourself. The better you connect and the better you communicate, the better you sell yourself to the individual or the audience.

Now that we know how important connecting is and what steps are needed to connect, it is time to dive into the techniques of effective communication and connecting, to save time, effort and to *Make More and Work Less*.

Find Desire and CONNECT!

Chapter 2 – Connect Through Desire

"Trust is the glue of life. It's the most essential ingredient in effective communication. It's the foundational principle that holds all relationships."

- Stephen Covey -

Assurance Keys to Connecting

- Communication Vs Connection

- How to Count Vs What Counts

- Why

- Goals

- Awareness

- Knowledge

- Interest

- Desire

- What is in it for (them)?

- Always look to add value.

MAKE MORE WORK LESS by CONNECTING

Chapter - 3 -
Connect Through Emotions

MAKE MORE WORK LESS by CONNECTING

Facts Tell; Emotions Sell

"How must this person feel so that this person will do what you want them to do?" – Nido Qubein

Do you believe that most people base their decisions on reason? logic? or facts? If you do, then you will find it difficult to understand why people make certain decisions. After long debates, arguments and discussions, you generally end up thinking that people making decisions (in your perspective) have …logically…bad reasoning. Reason, logic and facts, although have impact on decision making, are actually the smallest drivers of any decision being made. The strongest driver of all decisions is EMOTION.

Think back to when you were in school and you were preparing for an exam. Reason and logic will tell you that you SHOULD review and study regularly so that when the exam comes you will be prepared for it. However, knowing that the exam isn't until months later, you FEEL that you have the luxury of time on your side and therefore, put off the reviews and studying until later. On a day-to-day basis, you would never want or need to stay up all night to study, but when you realize that the exam is in two days and you haven't started studying, you are able to pull an all-nighter to study for the exam. But why did you do that? Is it because you really want to know the facts of what you are studying? Or is it the fear of failing the exam? The fear of not passing the course? In most cases it is the fear that will keep you up to study.

Look at what you are wearing right now. Why did you buy the shirt you are wearing? Or why did you decide to wear that shirt today? Is it because of the percentage of cotton in the material? Is it because of the type of thread that was used to

MAKE MORE WORK LESS by CONNECTING

put the shirt together? Is it the fact that it has a 2-inch collar verses a 2.5-inch collar? OR is it because you feel good in that shirt? Because it was a gift from a loved one? Or was it the shirt that was easiest to reach for so that you do not need to worry about what to wear? In most cases, again the decision to wear that shirt is based on a feeling and not a fact.

You may be thinking that these are very trivial cases, but when BIG decisions are made, they are made with reason. If that was the case, then I will ask how you decided which house you wanted to buy. The material, location, and size are all reasonable drivers, but were they reasonable because your feelings made it reasonable? Was the house the most logical option based on pricing or did you justify the pricing because you loved the house?

An astonishing study was done that shows how it is in our nature to follow our emotions rather than reason no matter how logical the facts or reasons are. This study was explained in the book *Freakonomics* by economist Steve Levitt.

> *The study is the economics of penalty kicks in soccer. At the elite level of soccer, 75 percent of the penalty kicks go in the net. At 80 mph the goalkeeper will not have enough time to react after the kick, and therefore, will need to make a decision prior to the kick as to where they will go. The kicker will always want to increase the likelihood of scoring even if the odds are already in his or her favour. If the goalkeeper guesses wrong the chances of the kicker scoring goes up to 90 percent. Based on statistics most players have a stronger right leg and therefore the chances of*

MAKE MORE WORK LESS by CONNECTING

the kicker kicking the ball to the left corner (goalkeepers right) is higher.

Sure, enough based on statistics the goalkeepers will generally guess to the left side of the goal 57 percent of the time versus 41 percent to the right side. If this is the case, then that means the middle is vacant 98 percent of the time! Evidently, of all the shots that were kicked toward the middle, 83 percent of them scored, yet only 17 percent of shots are aimed to the middle.

Why is that? Based on the facts, reason, and logic, wouldn't it make the most sense to aim down the middle when the goalkeeper is likely not going to be there? It comes down to the potential emotions of the kicker. The left corner or right corner kicks are the most difficult shots. If the kicker misses, the fans and spectators will reason that it was a tough shot and be forgiving. If the goalkeeper saves the shot, then the fans and spectators all will reason that the goalkeeper made a great save and be forgiving. However, if the kicker aims right down the middle and by chance the goalkeeper stops it without needing to move, then the fans and spectators will argue that the kicker didn't even try or even challenge the goalkeeper and will not be forgiving.

It is that feeling of ridicule and humiliation that kickers want to avoid and therefore, even with all the stats and all the logic they will still lean towards their emotions and take the lower percentage (yet still good odds) shot than the higher percentage shot.

MAKE MORE WORK LESS by CONNECTING

This demonstrates that it is truly how we feel that governs everything that we do. If our emotions dictate our decisions and our actions, then, in turn, how must our audience feel for them to receive the message and the information, or to do what we would like them to do? The moment we are able to engage with our audience emotionally, is the moment we have connected with them.

Who are you Connecting With?

For us to be able to connect with the audience emotionally we must understand who they are. Talking to a group of high school kids would be very different than talking to a group of successful entrepreneurs. The choice of words are different, type of stories that you can share are different, and the amount of emotion that you exert is different. Each time you speak will be different based on the audience members. Always find information about the audience as a group or the individual you are meeting ahead of time if possible.

Building rapport and a relationship with who you are talking is very important. There may be past similarities like growing up in the same city or playing the same sport; current similarities like kids and travel destinations. Knowing your audience allows you to pull references that are relatable and use language that resonates with the audience. For example, your encounter with Adam West (played the 1966 TV Batman) could be a great story with a group of comic enthusiasts, but it would not be with a group of entrepreneurs who would rather hear about your encounter with former Disney CEO Michael Eisner. Even simple items like word choice goes a long way when you know who the audience members are. Should you use language that is more proper versus informal? Would technical jargon work with a specific group or should the information be structured in a day-to-day perspective? These options come from knowing your audience. The better you know your audience the better you can speak and get your message out effectively and *Make More and Work Less*.

Know your Audience

Walt Disney is a master at knowing his audience. During the World War, the United States had a difficult time collecting taxes from their citizens. To solve this problem, the government decided to hire Walt Disney and have him create a cartoon that will encourage citizens to pay their taxes. Understanding the feelings of the citizens, Walt Disney created the animation short: *The New Spirit* (1942). This animation short features Donald Duck (representing the citizens of the United States) unmotivated to pay taxes. However, this was by no means due to him not being patriotic. During the film, it was explained to Donald Duck that paying taxes was easy, patriotic, and also supports the troops that were fighting overseas. After the government officials saw this short, they were disappointed and rejected the film saying that they did not like the character of Donald Duck and that they wanted a new character called "Mr. Taxman" for instance. Walt Disney refused to change his film stating that the citizens can relate to Donald Duck and that of all the characters that he can use, Donald Duck is the best option to reach out to the citizens and connect with them emotionally. Sure enough, after the airing of the film, tax payments went up by 30 percent! Illustrating the importance of knowing your audience.

Be in their Shoes

A great strategy in understanding your audience and connecting with the members is to be in their shoes. We have all been to lectures, concerts or movies at some point in our lives, and we are able to come out of these scenarios thinking: *"Wow that was really engaging!"* or *"That was so boring I fell asleep!"* So, with what you are planning on achieving think first as to how your audience will react. Would you be engaged in your presentation if you were in the audience? How would you need to speak, move, and look, for you to be interested in your performance? If your audience is made up of a group of children, think back to how you would feel when you were a child, what was on your mind, what were your interests? In contrast if your audience is a group of entrepreneurs, imagine what they would be interested in, attend seminars that they would attend prior to your presentation, and get a sense of their language and lives.

One of the best ways to gain new and different perspectives is to travel. With different cultures, different backgrounds and different environments, there are a lot of aspects that one would find odd or impossible, yet it is part of other's everyday lives. At times in North America, I would encounter situations that I would think that the person in front of me was an incompetent poor driver. I'm sure we have all felt that way one or two times in our lives. However, after a trip to Asia, I realized that I too can quickly become the said "incompetent" driver. I for one would never be able to drive in that traffic. I would be stuck at the merge lane hoping to get in it, all while having droves of cars behind me honking away telling me to go!

MAKE MORE WORK LESS by CONNECTING

Imagine this: What should be a four-lane road would, in reality, be five lanes or sometimes even six lanes. As you are driving through this mess, you need to avoid the street vendors on the side trying to sell you merchandise. Sticking bottles of water in your face or waving pineapples at your passengers. Not only that, there would frequently be a homeless person in the middle of this four-five-six lane road asking for a handout.

To top it all, intermingled among the cars, vendors, and beggars on the road are these scooters, and these are not just regular scooters, they are magic scooters! Why are they magic? Well, somehow what I thought should be a one-person ride (or at the very most two) can fit seven people, sometimes even 10! But wait, there's more! The passengers would be carrying groceries, air conditioners, or panes of glass. You name it they carry it.

Now, here is the kicker, there is no such thing as shoulder checking. There is an unwritten rule that whatever happens behind you is not your problem. You want to merge into a lane? Go ahead. Just go. People behind you will let you in it. As I'm stuck there in traffic, with drivers honking at me, I have now become the "incompetent" driver.

From that moment, I realized that perspective is a very important aspect in understanding people and situations. When you have that understanding, then you will be able to connect effectively with better choice of words, language, and style of speaking.

Give them an Experience

Once you have a general idea as to who your audience is, you will now be able to speak to their emotions.

- What makes them happy?
- What make them excited?
- What makes them sad?
- What make them fearful?
- What are they confident in?
- What are they weak in?
- What are their goals and aspirations?
- What are they looking for?

All these questions lead to a feeling, your job now is to trigger those emotions and have them feel those emotions by reaching for their past experiences and memories. This will require some creativity on your part. Depending on the message you want to get across or what you want your audience to do will determine what experiences you want them to feel. Let them feel what you feel.

For instance, if you were networking and wanted to make sure a good relationship is formed, then you may want to focus on topics that make the person you are talking to, feel good and comfortable, such as vacation destinations, family, and their greatest achievements. By doing so, they will have the memory of a great conversation with you and would likely meet up with you again.

In contrast, if you were on stage talking to a group of parents about a great investment, you may want topics that tap into their fear, like their lack of financial security or topics that allow them to picture a relaxing retirement where their kid's tuitions and their homes are paid for.

Four Drivers of Emotions

There are four main drivers that causes people to take action, to respond, or to feel a certain way: Gain, Fear, Pride, and Imitation. Depending on what your message is or what your purpose is when communicating with the individual or the audience, the four main drivers may vary in their effectiveness.

> **Gain** – Many people are driven by gain, something they want or need. They envision what it would be like to have something that they do not have. For instance, a business entrepreneur may tell their prospective partner all the benefits of a partnership, all the potential monetary gain, contacts and leads to be gained.
>
> **Fear** – Fear is one of the most powerful drivers. People respond to the fear of loss, the fear of pain, the fear of the unknown, etc. As Nido Qubein says: "People are fearful of change until the pain of remaining the same is greater than the pain of change". Just think back to when your parents told you why you had to study for school. Did a part of you feel the fear of being grounded that motivated you to study? Or the fear of failing that gave you that extra boost to study more? As long as it is ethical, fear is a great motivator when you are delivering your message. For instance, a coach may tell his team that if they do not work harder and learn the benefits of

MAKE MORE WORK LESS by CONNECTING

teamwork, then they will never fulfill their goal of winning a championship – the fear of losing.

Pride – At some point, we all enjoy feeling good about ourselves. When we accomplish a task, when we win in a race, or when we do well in an exam, we feel a sense of pride. That feeling stays with us and we draw upon it when we want to achieve our next goal. For example, a charity group may focus on the message of leaving a legacy and all the people that you can help with your donation. The act of helping others and being remembered by others will provide you a feeling of pride for doing an honorable thing.

Imitation – Have you ever felt alone? We all want to be a part of something, a part of a group, and to be included. In doing so, we are imitating what others are doing, how they are acting, what they are buying etc. As the saying goes "Keeping up with the Joneses". Imitation is a driver that many retail companies use to have people buy their products. The fact that everyone has a smart phone causes people who do not, to feel left out and want to get one themselves. As an example, to encourage more listeners to call in for a contest, a radio host would say that everyone will be at this concert, the concert is all sold out, or the only way to get tickets is to call in and enter the contest!

MAKE MORE WORK LESS by CONNECTING

Have stories, visuals, and surprises for all types of emotional experiences that would make your connection with your audience stronger, especially those that trigger the feelings of gain, fear, pride, and imitation. In the following chapter, you will be introduced to skills and techniques that will assist you in enhancing your ability to trigger your audience's emotions. Whether it is in structure, body gestures, vocal variety, and passion, you will soon realize that it is the combination of all the skills and techniques that make your communication most powerful.

Find out who you are connecting with.

MAKE MORE WORK LESS by CONNECTING

Chapter 3 – Connect Through Emotions

"To effectively communicate, we must realize that we are all different in the way we perceive the world and use this understanding as a guide to our communication with others."

- Tony Robbins -

Assurance Keys to Connecting

- Facts Tell; Emotions Sell

- How must one feel first.

- Who are you talking to?
    - Know your audience

- Be in their shoes
    - Understand where they are coming from.

- Give them an experience they won't forget.
    - Have them live through you.

- Top four emotional drivers
    - Gain
    - Fear
    - Pride
    - Imitation

MAKE MORE WORK LESS by CONNECTING

Chapter - 4 -
Connect Through Senses

MAKE MORE WORK LESS by CONNECTING

Bring It All Together

We now understand the difference between communicating and connecting, seeing versus observing, hearing versus listening, and words versus writing. We understand that to connect, to communicate effectively, and to get our message across to others, we must have the audience engaged emotionally and have them feel how we feel. However, it is always easier to understand the "theory" behind something than to "do" it. How do we make our communication more effective and more engaging? If we wanted to *Make More and Work Less,* we must be able to get our message across in the most effective way. You will soon discover that to do so, is a combination of many elements. From structure to body movements, to choice of words, to imagination, all working together to allow you to *Make More Work Less by Connecting.*

Structure

Think of the time when you were in school and you were asked to do a speech in front of a class or write an essay. How did you feel? How did you approach the task? Did you have a sense of panic? Did you do it last-minute? Did you have a system? During my time in school, I remember two very daunting tasks regarding essay writing:

> 1. Write a 4000 words paper (which now having authored a few books no longer seems such a daunting task) and
>
> 2. Complete three strong essays in 2.5 hours.

MAKE MORE WORK LESS by CONNECTING

4000 words!!?? 2.5 hours!!?? 150 mins!!?? At the time, those tasks seemed insurmountable! Then I remembered that I had a secret weapon -- five techniques that will allow me to come up with effective essays fast. Later, I realized that a 4000-word paper or writing books, is no different than having multiple essays combined together to support an overarching topic. Ultimately, speaking effectively is no different than structuring your thoughts the same way you would with an essay or paper.

The six techniques are: chronologically; the three Ts; power of threes and fives; funnel in, funnel out; what/so what/now what; and storytelling. Each technique has its purpose and effectiveness. However, when you combine a few of them, you will find how powerful structure is for effective communication.

Chronologically

This method is the easiest to adapt. It is basically following a timeline with dates, years, events, etc. This is the most effective way to illustrate historical events, backgrounds of individuals, and growth of companies and businesses.

Example:

> In 1901, an inspirational man, Walt Disney, was born. At the age of 18, Walt was employed at Posman-Rubin Art Studio. In 1924, Disney Brothers Studio was formed. Four years later, Mickey Mouse was created during a train ride. On July 13, 1955, Disneyland opened its doors.

MAKE MORE WORK LESS by CONNECTING

The Three T's

In most talks, there is an opening, body, and closing. Usually, this is separated by an introduction, supporting points and a conclusion. The Three T's are: **T**ell them what you are about to tell them, **T**ell them, and **T**ell them what you just told them. Basically, in your introduction, you will tell your audience what you are about to tell them. In your body sections, you will be telling them. And finally, you will tell them what you just told them in a summary during your conclusion. By doing so, you will have a lasting impact on your audience.

Example:

> *Intro - The animation industry was revolutionized by one very inspirational individual, Walt Disney. By looking at his career as a cartoonist, as an innovator, and a storyteller, it is obvious that without Disney, animation would not be where it is today.*
>
> *Body 1 - As a cartoonist...*
>
> *Body 2 - Not only was his work as a cartoonist revolutionary but also his innovations while developing his films was well before it's time...*
>
> *Body 3 - Ultimately, one can see that it is Walt's ability to tell stories that united his passion for cartooning and innovating.*
>
> *Conclusion – After understanding how Walt Disney was as a cartoonist, an innovator, and most importantly as a storyteller at heart, it is obvious that if*

MAKE MORE WORK LESS by CONNECTING

not for Walt Disney, animation would be years behind and nowhere near what we experience today.

The Power of Threes and Fives

Depending on the length of time that you are allotted, whether it is an impromptu interview question or a formal keynote presentation, always attempt to stick to odd numbers. If you are asking questions at the beginning of a talk, ask three questions. When giving support information, give three, five, or seven supporting points. When repeating information, repeat it three times. The human brain responds to triplets a lot more than doubles. Just think of when we were kids, and your parents told you to clean your room. If you didn't do it the first time it was asked, you probably did it after the third time because, after the third time, there may be consequences. When we get ready for a race it is one, two, three, GO! When we knock on doors, we generally knock three times. The value of three also gives a sense of three levels: good-better-best, bad-worse-worst, beginning-middle-ending, strong-stronger-strongest! When used effectively, presenting information in triplets will get you the most impact.

Example:

> Questions – Who here has ever been touched by a cartoon? Have you ever wondered how animation advanced so quickly in such a short period of time? Have you ever wondered what animation would be like without the existence of Walt Disney?
>
> Points – Walt Disney's Cartooning (strong), Innovation (stronger), and Storytelling (strongest).

MAKE MORE WORK LESS by CONNECTING

Set your points up to have the greatest impact in the end. Leave a strong lasting impression on your audience. By asking questions, you will start off strong by creating curiosity in the audience.

Funnel In – Funnel Out

This technique basically tells you to envision your talk or paper as if there was a funnel on top and an upside-down funnel at the bottom. Your introduction will start in a general sense to engage as many audience members as possible. Asking questions or providing facts that relates to most of your audience. As you wind down your introduction, you get more specific, and into your main points of the body sections. After you are done your main points, you "funnel out" in your conclusion. This is where you summarize what you talked about specifically, then broaden it out again with generalization and questions and finally presenting a thought-provoking statement or challenge to give a lasting impression.

Example:

> Intro: (Generalize) see questions in the above section. (Funnel in) Tell them the specifics – Cartooning, Innovation, Storytelling
>
> Body Sections: (Specific)
>
> Conclusion: Summarize the three points (Specific - now Funnel out). We all have the ability to create, to innovate, and tell stories. In fact, we tell stories every day! Because we already do this, wouldn't you say that you too can make an impact on industry, people

MAKE MORE WORK LESS by CONNECTING

and loved ones that you see every day? What is one thing you can do more effectively if you were to improve on your storytelling skills? (Generalized)

What?/So What?/Now What?

What? So What? Now What? Can also be viewed as: Problem-Impact-Solution or Cause-Effect-Benefit. By having this format while structuring your talk or paper, you will stay on task and basically have a map to where you want to go with your message. This system works very well for impromptu speaking, networking, and interviews. It instantly gives you structure to your responses allowing you to present your thoughts and message.

Example 1:

> Question: Who inspires you?
>
> What/Who – Walt Disney
> So What/Why them – Cartooning, Innovation, Storytelling
> Now What/relate – I can tell stories, innovate, and inspire others too.

Example 2:

> Question: What is Leadership?
> What – Compassion, Decisiveness, and Equality
> So What – Examples of each
> Now What – We can all become better leaders if we focus on enhancing these qualities.

MAKE MORE WORK LESS by CONNECTING

Storytelling

Whether you are telling a story about someone else, a story you heard from somewhere else or a personal story, storytelling is the most powerful way to get your message across. It encompasses emotions, experiences, and engagement. This is a great way to combat impromptu situations and interviews. Giving personal stories/ experiences is easy because they are your stories, so you know them, and it allows you to speak conversationally. We will get into more details of storytelling later on in this book.

Example 1:

> *Body Sections: Story about Cartooning, Innovation, and Storytelling*

Example 2:

> *Body Sections: Story about Compassion, Decisiveness, and Equality*

Once you understand the six techniques: chronologically; the Three T's; Power of Threes and Fives; Funnel in, Funnel out; What/So What/Now What; and Storytelling you will be able to discover how combining them (as shown in parts in the above examples) will create a very powerful structured talk or paper or response that will leave you memorable, impactful, and most importantly have your message connect with the audience.

MAKE MORE WORK LESS by CONNECTING

SECRETS TO A POWERFUL SPEECH!

OPENING/INTRODUCTION

T-T-T
Tell them what you will tell them
Tell them
Tell them what you told them

FUNNEL IN

POWER OF 3's BODY

FUNNEL OUT

CLOSING/CONCLUSION

Funnel In – Opening:

Generalize – Engage and bring the audience in → Ask Questions, Quotes, Story

Relation – Can the Audience relate to your topic?

Focus - Funnel into your topic

Power of 3's – Body:

3 points

3 questions

3 supporting statements

Funnel Out – Conclusion:

Reinforce your point

Summarize your support

Generalize

Give the audience something to think about → Ask a question or have a call to action

Connecting VS Communication

Facts Tell – Emotion Sells

How must someone feel first so that they will do what you want them to do?

E-P-C

ENERGY – The **more energy** you give the more energy your audience will give back.
PASSION – The **more passion** you have the more engaged your audience will be.
CONFIDENCE – The **more confidence** you have the more success you will have.

MAKE MORE WORK LESS by CONNECTING

Reach for Their Senses

Close your eyes. Take a deep breath. Clear your mind. Think back to the last time you walked into a bakery. Remember the smell of fresh bread coming from the oven? Can you feel the warmth of the shop? The heat from the ovens? Now, pick up that freshly baked croissant and smell that buttery goodness. Can you feel the warmth in your hands? The crumbling of the pastry? As you take that first bite, remember the sensation of the freshness as you savor the moment. The crispiness of the outside balanced with the softness of the inside. It is so good!

Anyone want a freshly baked croissant right now? Everyone? Yeah, me too. When we speak to our audience or to an individual, think of ways to reach their senses. Our senses can be used to let others relate to something that can emphasize your message or point. And the best part of it is that your audience is doing it themselves! You are just guiding them along.

Notice when you see Starbucks ads or Tim Horton's commercials, you always see the steam rising from their coffee? So much so that you can almost smell the coffee? When Apple came out with the very first iPod, Steve Jobs did not talk about the storage space or casing. He said, "Imagine 1,000 songs in your pocket." When McDonalds advertises, they ask, "Have you had your break today?" These messages are sent to you with you visualizing yourself relaxing, feeling the warmth or convenience.

Likewise, if we wanted to have the most impact while speaking, we can connect most effectively by using descriptive words that triggers our audience's senses. Words such as: imagine, feel, experience, etc. can take them to a place in their minds. Then describe in detail what you want them to feel and sense. The clearer the picture you paint for them in their minds, the more senses (sight, taste, smell, sound, touch, and feel) you connect with, the more effective your message will be.

Body Speaks

A lot of us believe that what we say is the most important part of speaking. Therefore, we spend a lot of time perfecting how things are put together, what words to use, and what is the best supporting information. We stress ourselves out so much with "*What do I say? What do I say?*" that we are actually neglecting something far more important than the words that we want to say -- our body. The last thing we want to do is spend all that time and effort perfecting the words that we are going to say, only to fail to connect with the audience because of our body movements. Body movements includes everything from: arm gestures, movements around the area, head movements, eye contact, and facial expressions. According to studies 55 percent of communication is through body language, 38 percent is tone of voice (explained later) and only 7 percent are the words being used!

MAKE MORE WORK LESS by CONNECTING

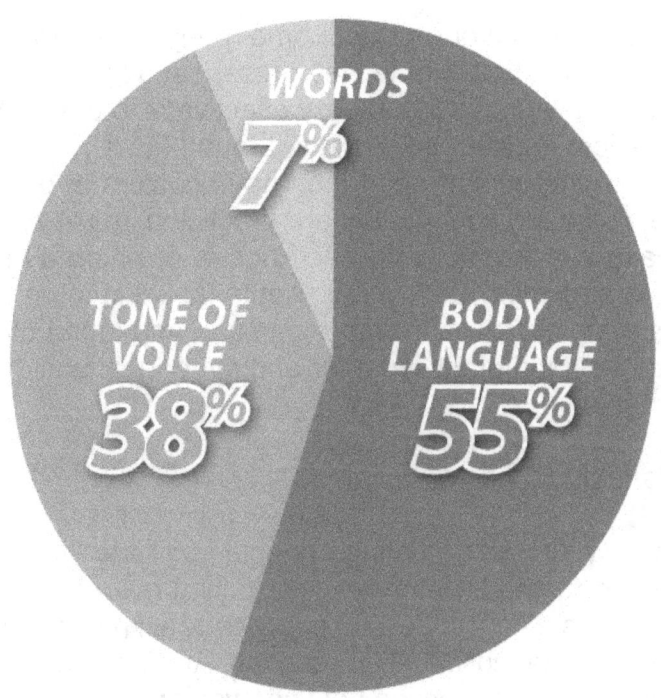

Eye Contact

Eye contact is probably the most important element of body language. It allows you to be engaged with your audience. It gives the audience the sense that you are talking to and acknowledging them. Having consistent eye contact also allows you a chance to see how your audience is reacting to the information that you are providing. Are they interested? Are they bored? Are they paying attention?

When it comes to eye contact there are many methods that one can implement to be more comfortable with making eye contact. A very common technique is to practice your speeches, presentations, or interviews in front of a mirror. Another is to practice in front of family, friends, and sometimes even your pets. Some people like to record themselves and watch how they present at a later time. One strategy that we have found very effective is to practice your presentation standing up, walking around (as if you were on stage or at the podium) and then have posters or photos of people all around you. As you are practicing, make sure that you make eye contact with each poster or photo as if they were the audience. One of our clients took this to heart and cut out people's faces from a magazine and taped them all over his wall and practiced over and over again until he was comfortable.

The Handshake

Whether you are meeting people for the first time, networking, going to interviews, or taking over a stage, the handshake is a very important element of acknowledging the audience or the individual's presence. At most times, this is the first physical interaction between you and your audience. Make sure your handshake is firm and full of confidence, none of those "dead fish" handshakes we all experience from time to time. While shaking hands, always make eye contact with the person. If they are important enough for you to shake hands, then they are important enough for you to give them your acknowledgement with eye contact. That eye contact signifies an unwritten "Thank you" message to the person giving you the opportunity to speak with them, for their time, or for their audience. If you are taking over the stage, the handshake shows the passing of the stage to you. It also shows professionalism to the audience seeing the interaction take place and the credibility of association with whom you shook hands. At the very least, the handshake is the first and easiest way to show respect to whom you are interacting.

MAKE MORE WORK LESS by CONNECTING

Facial Expressions

When you are describing emotions and feelings in your talk you should always have your facial expressions match the feelings that you want your audience to feel. You wouldn't talk about the greatest day of your life with a frown. You would do so with a great smile! Likewise, you wouldn't show facial expressions of fear or anger if you were trying to express confidence to your audience.

Body Gestures

Think of the last time you played charades. How did you use your hands? Your arms? How did you express BIG? How did you illustrate FAST? Similarly, while doing your talk, matching your body gestures to your words is very important. Even if certain words are missed, your gestures may be enough for your audience to fill in the blanks. If you want to show confidence then you would stand firmly with confidence. If you were telling a story of fear, you would show body gestures of being closed off and small. As the saying goes "*A picture is worth a thousand words*", so use your body to illustrate a picture to enhance your words.

Using the area in which you are speaking in also falls in the body gestures category. Using all the space will allow you to connect with audiences to the left and right of you. Using the back or front of the stage can allow you to create different effects or visuals for the audience. The better your stage presence is, the higher engagement you will receive from the audience.

MAKE MORE WORK LESS by CONNECTING

Hands

If eye contact is the most important element in the head area, then the hands would be the most important element of the rest of your body. Something as simple as how your hands are presented can give three completely different messages to your audience even when the words and tone are exactly the same.

For example, let's say we have the following instructions:

1) People in the back come to the front
2) The people in the front move over to the left
3) The people on the left move over to the back

Now give these instructions in the following three ways to someone you know: (Remember to keep the words the same and your tone and speed the same.)

1) Pointing at the people and locations with your index finger.

2) Pointing at the people and locations with an open palm, with the palm facing down.

3) Pointing at the people and locations with an open palm, with the palm facing up (like you were serving an item).

How did your partner feel? They would most likely be happier following your instructions when you did it the third way and not at all when you gave it the first way. The pointing index finger gives an offensive feel to the instructions while the open palm up method feels inviting and pleasant. The open

MAKE MORE WORK LESS by CONNECTING

palm down method feels like you are being talked down to but not offensive as being pointed at. Simple adjustments to the way you position your hands can change the effect of how your audience feels. A great example of this can be seen in the video by Allan Pease titled: *The Power is in the Palm of your Hands*, which can be seen online.

Another example as to why your hand gestures are so important is that there are many cultures integrated into our society, and certain gestures could be offensive in certain cultures. This is evident in all Disney Parks where it is a rule that all cast members who give directions, must do so with an open palm when asked. This is because, in some cultures, pointing with your index finger is offensive, and because Disney Parks welcomes guests from all over the world, they do not want to offend a guest by mistake, which may lead to a poor guest experience.

Vocal Variety

If you have perfected your structure, your body gestures, and your content, the last thing you want to do is deliver the entire talk without any vocal variety, which involves using highs and lows of inflection, fast and slow of speech throughout your talk. Imagine someone saying *"It was the time of my life..."* with a monotone style. Would you believe that it was *"The time of their life"* versus someone saying *"IT WAS THE TIME ...OF MY ...LIFE!!"* with emphasis on the words "TIME" and "LIFE"? Vocal variety is like painting a picture with sound, giving life to the words, giving the words feeling and depth. Now, you should not go overboard with this as you want the tone and the pacing to be congruent with your content and your audience.

MAKE MORE WORK LESS by CONNECTING

Visual Aids

To enhance your talk even further, you can have some sort of visual aid. According to the learning pyramid, simply having your content in point form for your audience to read increases the likelihood of them remembering from 5 percent to 10 percent. If you were to show an image, an object, or a demonstration of your message, your audience's retention goes up to 30 percent. Again… "*A picture is worth a thousand words.*" What can you provide your audience with visually so that you can use less words, less effort but provide more impact?

THE LEARNING PYRAMID

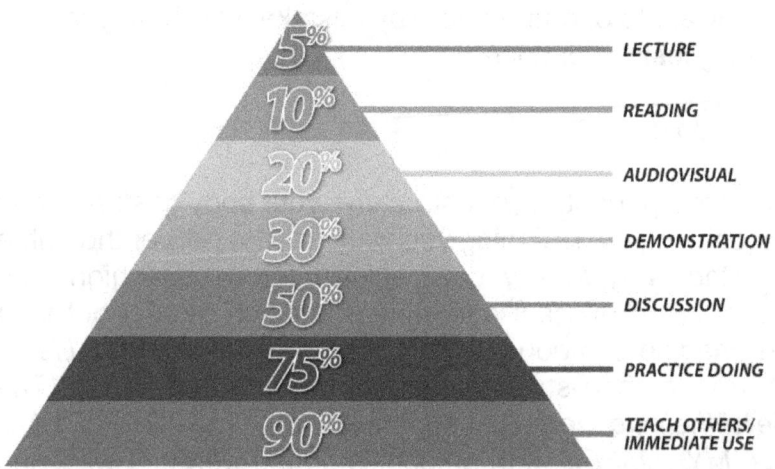

- 5% — LECTURE
- 10% — READING
- 20% — AUDIOVISUAL
- 30% — DEMONSTRATION
- 50% — DISCUSSION
- 75% — PRACTICE DOING
- 90% — TEACH OTHERS/ IMMEDIATE USE

For example think about how you would explain the game of chess to someone with words versus using diagrams and sketches. Or simply describing to someone what an elephant looks like with words rather than a photo. This is evident when we ask for directions. It is a lot more effective to have someone sketch out the path than to just tell you.

MAKE MORE WORK LESS by CONNECTING

An absolutely prime example of how body language, vocal variety, and visual aids impact your message and presentation can be found online with the video by Will Stephen titled: *How to Sound Smart in your TEDx Talk*. You will be amazed at how much you will learn from a talk about "Nothing"!

Passion

Ultimately, the key to effective communication and connecting is PASSION. You will soon realize that if you have an absolute strong passion about something, your gestures will automatically be relevant, your vocal variety will have the most effective emphasis on the right words, your pacing and your pauses will be natural. You will automatically think of visuals and methods to get your point across. The key is PASSION, as long as you speak passionately about your topic, your message or your opinion, people will listen. Whether your audience agree or disagree, know or have no idea about your topic, your passion will intrigue them enough to give you some attention. A passionate person explaining the life of a bee could make it a very entertaining topic while someone who is an expert in skydiving but was not passionate about it would explain it like a lecture making it boring and unbearable. No matter how dull a topic can be, if one was to talk about it with utmost passion, it can be interesting. When a topic or message is interesting then the audience will pay attention and, at the very least, your message will be heard.

A great example of how passion can lead to success can be seen through a season of the TV series *The Celebrity Apprentice*. Matt Iseman, the host of the show Ninja Warrior, went into the competition as the underdog. However, due to

MAKE MORE WORK LESS by CONNECTING

his passion for his charity, his passion can be seen in his participation, his work, his energy, and his presentations. It was his passion that allowed him to be successful and a great competitor in the show.

By looking at how to structure effectively, use body language, use vocal variety, know your audience, and tap into your passion, it is obvious that these elements will allow you to connect with your audience with ease. Using these techniques can make it easier for you when you want to have your message heard and understood. Being able to connect with your audience and emotionally get them engaged will make it a lot easier for you to *Make More and Work Less*, saving you time, effort, and stress. What we have described in this chapter is but a small sample of the skills, techniques, and methods that are used to become an effective communicator. Organizations such as Toastmasters and Dale Carnegie are great places to start honing your skills. To speed up the process, hiring a coach or registering in effective speaking workshops are other options for you to fine tune and have specific areas improved.

In the following few chapters we will look at how effective communication and connecting affected the success of a variety of experts and professionals in their respective fields. Through their experiences and journeys, it is evident that there is one main thing in common: The importance of effective communication. Effective communication is something everyone needs to improve on. When you can connect with your audience and other individuals, relationships develop and success comes naturally.

MAKE MORE WORK LESS by CONNECTING

MAKE MORE WORK LESS by CONNECTING

Chapter 4 – Connect Through Senses

"Take advantage of every opportunity to practice your communication skills so that when important occasions arise, you will have the gift, the style, the sharpness, the clarity, and the emotions to affect other people."
- Jim Rohn -

Assurance Keys to Connecting

- Structure and Organize
    - TTT; funnel in, funnel out
    - What, So What, Now What

- Power of Threes and Fives

- Storytelling

- Speak to their senses.

- 55 percent of effective communication is body language.

- Eye contact and hands are key elements.

- Vocal Variety

- Visual Aids

- PASSION

MAKE MORE WORK LESS by CONNECTING

Chapter - 5 -

Teaching Connects

By Gloria Bosma

"Because the purpose of this book is to showcase the importance of effective communication, we thought about who we know who would need to communicate effectively daily. Most importantly, what professions will need to communicate effectively at all times, because it is vital to their success? We asked ourselves, "Who in our lives have shown us the way to succeed and to Make More and Work Less?" It is our coaches, mentors, and teachers! So, it became evident that we had to get the thoughts of a lifelong teacher who has helped shape the minds of many children and many more generations to come. She is someone who makes learning fun but also adds effective communication into her teachings so that her students are set for success. Therefore, it was a no brainer to start this section off with the teacher who finds your inner spark --Gloria Bosma."

MAKE MORE WORK LESS by CONNECTING

MAKE MORE WORK LESS by CONNECTING

Making a Difference

"We are going to work on a class mural except for you, Gloria."

"I see you have a passion for science, so I bought you this biochemistry book. You might not be able to read all the words right now, but I hope that one day it will spark something in you."

These words were spoken by two teachers - neither of them realizing their simple words would make such a difference in my life. One teacher's words caused me to view myself as having zero artistic ability, the other carved a path for my career as a Science Teacher.

As teachers, we are role models, the voice of reason and guidance. One misstep can have a catastrophic effect on a student's future. Conversely, if it is done effectively then the impact on that child's future is limitless. Therefore, being able to communicate as a teacher effectively is not only vital to our success as a teacher but also the success and future of the student.

I have had the privilege of teaching students from Kindergarten to 6th grade, at the university level and have home-schooled my son. These experiences allow me to see education from a unique lens. I am truly passionate about igniting the spark in each child and watching this spark fan into a flame. It excites me to see students who walk in during September feeling like they have little to offer, and watch them leave in June as skilled and confident individuals. As a teacher, one of my greatest rewards is connecting with former students and hearing the difference I made in their lives. Moments like these are priceless.

Knowing that our words can make a **profound** difference in the lives of others, we need to communicate effectively to students with varying abilities from countries around the globe, many with limited English skills. Is it possible to communicate the wonder of the world around us and the value of each student placed in our care? I believe that it is imperative that we do a good job of this because words can have a huge impact on a person.

Love and Value

"What a teacher is, is more important than what she teaches."
- Karl Meninger

What a powerful quote to remind us that not only do our students learn from our prepared lessons, but through every encounter they have with us.

What do we communicate as a student walks through our door? Do we communicate, "*I am so glad that you are here*", or "*Hurry up so that I can start my lesson.*" Which approach might yield better results?

I believe that in teaching, two very important elements are: Respect and Value. As teachers we must show how much we care for and value our students. It is when that love and appreciation is felt that trust is formed. When there is trust, our message is heard loud and clear. It truly is the biggest piece of teaching. Communication with a student is no different than communication with a spouse, a business partner, or a potential client, it is important in all our lives.

MAKE MORE WORK LESS by CONNECTING

"I've learned that people will forget what you said and what you did. But people will never forget how you made them feel."
- Maya Angelou

How do you make your students feel? A good place to begin is by knowing who your students are. What are they passionate about? How did their game go? What did they do as a family? Do you show students that you value them through nonverbal communication cues – a smile, a nod, getting down to their level, hand on a shoulder, or do your students see that "teacher look" when they aren't performing? We all know that look, don't we? Trust me, you can definitely *"Make More and Work Less"*, once you have invested time in getting to know what drives each student and showing that you genuinely care.

How does this play out in an office setting? Do you take the time to truly communicate with colleagues you spend eight hours a day with? How tragic that some individuals can get so wrapped up in "work" that they neglect to afford their colleagues the courtesy of a cordial greeting. Make a point of truly engaging with those around you. Notice them, find out about their likes, their family, their dreams. Create a culture in your work environment where people can truly enjoy each other's company.

As in every organization, it is important to establish a positive working environment. Students need to be able to interact with each other in a healthy manner. As a teacher, my job is to model these skills. Do I truly listen when my students speak to me after the umpteenth time of who did what to whom on the playground? How do I communicate when things are not going as planned?

MAKE MORE WORK LESS by CONNECTING

Another important element of communication is delivering information in a way that students are excited about learning. I tend to be quite animated in class. I truly believe that if you can show how excited you are about something, it becomes contagious.

"...Mrs. Bosma's job is to teach science, but she lets us have lots of fun instead. No, she teaches us fun science, that's why she is No.1!"
- Joanne

Students are so unique and learn in a multitude of ways. It is very important to communicate in ways that help them make connections. This could mean dramatizing a concept, coming up with a song, challenging them to research a question, inviting guest speakers, connecting with others, spending one-to-one time - anything that can help students forge a connection. We need to do whatever it takes to reach and teach each child.

A very powerful communication tool that I implement is the *"Chair of Awesomeness"*. Very simply, a student sits in a chair and each member of the class shares what he or she appreciates about that student. It is amazing to see the difference that verbal affirmation makes. Someone could come in having the worst day and leave feeling like they are on top of the world. Can you imagine what companies would look like if they implemented the *"Chair of Awesomeness?"* Make a point of verbally affirming people in your everyday life. You may never know how important a few kind words may mean.

A question was asked of me as to what I do when things don't quite turn out as they should. I can think of a lot of times when

MAKE MORE WORK LESS by CONNECTING

something did not turn out the way it should – water all over a student, something that burned -- the list goes on. These moments are the ones that kids are going to remember the most. Sometimes, more important than the incident, is our reaction to it. Humour is a great antidote for the bloopers in life.

Recently, my students were able to follow my journey as I competed at various speech competitions. They were able to cheer me on as I won three competitions and hear about my eventual loss. No, it didn't turn out the way I had hoped, but what a great lesson to show that we need to be able to accept both the wins and the losses in life, allowing both to teach and propel us forward.

In teaching, not only do we need to communicate with students, but also with parents, colleagues, and administrators. Communication with parents generally happens via e-mail or direct conversation. If parents come to me with a concern, I frame the concern around the notion that the parents truly care about their children and want what is best for them. Framing my response by beginning and ending with acknowledging this, allows the parents to know that we both care about their children, creating a more receptive atmosphere.

Parents tend to receive phone calls from teachers when things aren't going well. That is why it is important to pick up the phone and share when there is also good news. Who wouldn't want to hear that their child had a really great day?

It is imperative that students know how to resolve conflict through effective communication. Usually, a situation involves hurt feelings about what someone else did or said.

MAKE MORE WORK LESS by CONNECTING

Both parties are brought together with the goal of resolving the situation, repairing the relationship and learning better methods of communicating.

When you care for someone, you do everything you can to help that person succeed. You spend the time explaining concepts, you find different ways of making it easier to understand, and you give it more energy to make it fun. When conflict occurs, you spend that extra time asking the right questions and finding the right solutions for all parties involved. Communicating effectively is easier when you put your heart into it, have the other person's best interest in mind and find some common ground.

We All Start Somewhere

Throughout the years, I have had students and parents comment on my communication skills and thank me for teaching these to the younger generation. It is gratifying to see students exude confidence while delivering a speech or reading orally. This was far from my experience as a child. I remember when I was a young student being so shy that I could not even put up my hand to go to the bathroom.

In my adult years, a friend of mine asked me to share my experiences in Mongolia. I pictured a few friends around a coffee table and thought – why not? Little did I know that I would be standing in front of a lectern with a microphone and a room full of women. I was mortified! My voice went dry and crackled, my hands shook so much that I could barely hold on to the microphone. Somehow, I made it through without anyone having to do CPR on me, and, at that point, I realized that I needed to work on my fear of public speaking.

MAKE MORE WORK LESS by CONNECTING

I joined a Toastmasters Club, which was instrumental in improving my communication skills. Through Toastmasters, I was able to learn the necessary skills in becoming an effective communicator, which, in turn, helped me gain confidence. What was especially helpful is a segment of the meetings called Table Topics. This is where members are asked to answer impromptu questions on the spot, allowing us to develop our ability to think and speak fast on our feet.

Because of my childhood fear of public speaking, I do everything possible to ensure that my students are equipped with the necessary skills to become effective communicators and leaders. If you come into my classroom and ask who wants to read or deliver a speech, nearly every hand will shoot up, which is so unlike my experience growing up.

Adam gives us an insight into what made the difference for him.

"When Mrs. Bosma asked me to do Table Topics, I didn't want to do it at all because I was so scared. I thought I would be humiliated, and everyone would laugh at me. When I did get up, everyone clapped so loud for me and told me all the things that I did great and how I could improve. It made me feel so good. Now, I want to be the first one up there. I really love it and wish we could do it all the time."
- Adam

Attitude is key. If an individual feels capable, they will continue to work at a skill, which will, in turn, improve his or her performance level. I have seen the results.

"Praise, like sunlight, helps all things grow."
- Croft M. Pentz

MAKE MORE WORK LESS by CONNECTING

Leadership opportunities are also important, especially for those students who seldom have this opportunity. I chose two young men to be emcees at a recent school assembly. A fellow teacher came up to me afterward and said, *"When I saw who you chose as emcees I thought, 'What are they going to do up there?'"* These two young men wowed the entire school. I overheard a conversation where one of the boys asked, *"Are you jealous of me?"* They both shared how these experiences gave them confidence they never had, and they have come to realize they are very capable of something they thought was impossible. Equally endearing was one of the parents who was nearly in tears as she shared, *"For the first time, I feel hopeful that my son actually has skills."*

"A good teacher can inspire hope, ignite the imagination, and instill a love of learning."
- Brad Henry

From the shy girl who found it difficult to make eye contact, I have had the opportunity to hold numerous leadership positions and am comfortable delivering keynotes, facilitating workshops, and speaking to a variety of audiences. This happened because I invested in improving my communication and leadership skills. Opportunities open as we develop our skills, and each opportunity allows us to grow. In fact, I continue to challenge myself as I compete in speech competitions, something the little girl who would not put her hand up in class would never have dreamed of doing.

Not only are opportunities opening for myself but also by imparting communication skills to my son, it has created so many experiences and life-changing moments for him as well! My son, Brandon, has Mosaic Trisomy 18, which is an

MAKE MORE WORK LESS by CONNECTING

extra chromosome on the 18th chromosome. Trisomy18 is labelled "lethal" and because of this, children with this diagnosis are generally denied medical services.

Brandon is working at changing the dialogue around current medical practices and saving lives by spreading his message. With the skills of delivering an effective message and being someone who is deeply tied to the message, he has had the opportunity of delivering a keynote address in Tacoma, Washington, a Ted X Youth talk, Canadian Physicians for Life Conference, Pediatric Grand Rounds, Disability Equipping Conference, Year two medical students at the University of Alberta, Global News Health Matters, CBC news and radio, and several junior and senior high schools. He has also created numerous videos. One that he downloaded a few months ago has garnered more than 18,000 views. Brandon also has his own Web site and Facebook page, all of which require great communication skills. Oh, and did I mention that he did all this while being diagnosed with a 58 IQ, ADD, and sensory issues?

Luckily for him, or perhaps unluckily for him, he has a Mama who is passionate about this area. We have been moved to tears on many occasions by heartfelt e-mails from parents around the globe who have been given hope by a video or a talk. One recent e-mail ended by saying:

"I hope one day that I will be able to meet you in person and shake your hand to let you know what you have done for me and my family. Brandon, you are our hero."
- Michael

Knowing that we are making a difference in the world is huge. That is the power of effective communication. Being able to reach out, deliver a message that moves you and impact others to show that they are not alone and have the support when they need it.

You Have an Important Message

When going on stage to deliver a speech or a talk to one, five or several hundred, I find that as long as you truly believe that your message is important and that the people in the audience will gain value from your talk, then everything else will fall into place. Your energy will be there, your body language will follow suit and your authenticity will show. Having said that, one can never forget to practice until you feel confident in your delivery. That will allow you to have a good base in case something does not go according to plan.

Finally, one very important thought before you do your speech or talk is that it is 100 percent about the audience. It is not about you. You are there to add value to the audience, so focus on that aspect. When your mind is on helping others, it alleviates some of the pressure.

Everyone Needs to Communicate

No matter what your future holds you will need to communicate in one shape or form. By being a teacher, I am passing on the skills of effective communication to the younger generation because that is the one skill that will open countless doors of opportunity. I totally understand fear. I was there. I believe the key is to not let the voice of fear prevent you from moving forward. Learn the necessary skills and put them into practice. Remember that one small step at a time is the key.

MAKE MORE WORK LESS by CONNECTING

If someone like Brandon, who must work so hard at delivering a speech can do it, there is no reason that you cannot do it. By saying yes, he is making a difference in the world, what would your yes do for you? Effective communication is such a key component in our workplace and personal relationships. If we can learn to do this well, our world will be a better place.

If you would like to follow Brandon's journey, you may connect with him at www.brandonsmt18journey.com and at www.facebook.com/BrandonsMosaicTrisomy18Journey/

MAKE MORE WORK LESS by CONNECTING

Chapter 5 – Teaching Connects

"Communication is a skill that you can learn. It's like riding a bicycle or typing. If you're willing to work at it, you can rapidly improve the quality of every part of your life."

- Brian Tracy -

Assurance Keys to Connecting

- Effective communication opens opportunities.

- Focus on Love and Value.

- Communicate how much you appreciate others.

- Show genuine care for other people – build relationships.

- Have the other person's best interest in mind.

- Find common ground.

- You have an important message.

- It is 100 percent about the audience, not you.

- What will your "Yes" do for you?

MAKE MORE WORK LESS by CONNECTING

MAKE MORE WORK LESS by CONNECTING

Chapter - 6 -

Community Connects
By Glenda Sheard

*"Whether it is entertainment, investments or education, connecting with your audience, makes everything go more smoothly. When that connection is achieved in the community, then the results are astronomical! How can one Make More and Work Less by Connecting with the community? Well, when fundraising for a cause, connecting with your donors and building relationships within your community will help to ensure success in your fundraising efforts. The more relationships and partnerships that are built, the higher the potential of more funds that can be raised. To find out more about connecting with the community, we reached out to a master fundraiser, a person full of passion, a speaker and coach, and an individual who pours her heart into everything she does -- Glenda Sheard. She has helped hundreds of youth and young adults build their confidence in becoming better communicators. She has also raised millions of dollars for nonprofit organizations. We are pleased to introduce our fundraiser expert, Glenda Sheard of **A Compassionate Tomorrow** to share with us some strategies as to how we can better connect with our audiences."*

MAKE MORE WORK LESS by CONNECTING

MAKE MORE WORK LESS by CONNECTING

Importance of Effective Communication

Every person needs to be able to communicate. Whether it be in our relationships with our colleagues at work or with our relationships with family and friends, communication is a vital skill. The more effective of a communicator that we become, the more effective we are at interacting with those around us. As we go about our lives, we also interact and communicate with others in our community; as volunteers, mentors and coaches, neighbours or even a casual conversation with a stranger. Communication is imperative in every relationship that we have. I also believe that we are all given opportunities to be servant leaders in our communities. With all our relationships, the stronger we are as communicators, the stronger relationships we can build. Effective communication is reached when we truly "connect" with another individual, a group of people or a large audience.

Furthermore, enhancing our communication skills, also enhances our leadership skills. Regardless of any conditions, every person is born to be a leader in one form or another.

Passion is the Key

To connect with your audience, the first and foremost element is PASSION! In my case, it is of utmost importance to communicate and connect with current donors and potential donors. Within the community, I am known for my passion to help make a difference for others. As a fundraiser for Strathcona County Library, I am incredibly passionate about literacy. When your passion is directly related to the charity that you are fundraising for, it makes the connection to your audience that much easier. Your excitement and energy are clearly evident as you speak about your cause. When you speak with confidence, you can speak to anyone that will listen to you. Why? Because your passion for the cause comes straight from your heart. When you speak with energy, authenticity, and passion, people will listen. That is where my success in fundraising stems from – Passion.

I love to share that same passion when working or volunteering with youth. I have an immense passion to assist youth in building their confidence and communication skills. One of my greatest reward in working with youth and young adults is when I witness how they grew in their confidence, and how they enhanced their communication and leadership skills. There is no greater gift than to see a young person that once lacked confidence, to now stand up straighter with pride, feeling empowered, and knowing they have the tools to succeed. They have stronger articulation in their speaking, they *"Listen Louder"* (listen more effectively), and they have the skills to evaluate and assess situations much better. Watching young people gain the most effective skillset they will ever need in their lives, the art of communication, fuels my passion with every young person that I meet.

Whether it is fundraising for a cause or working with youth in the community, communicating and connecting are a must and passion is the key!

Empowering Passion – Listening Louder

Now, passion will get you part way there. At the very least, you will have the attention of your audience. One must then structure that passion strategically and effectively to connect with the audience. We would all like to believe that we are effective communicators, however there will come a time when you start asking yourself *"How come they didn't*

MAKE MORE WORK LESS by CONNECTING

donate? How come less donations came? Why didn't this young person improve in their communication?" The reasons can be endless. Sure, it can be the economy, the individual, the timing, and so on. However, it will likely be due to your ineffective communication or lack of connecting. Unlike all the other reasons that you may come up with, enhancing your communication skills is one thing that you can have control over. So why not take charge?

A true moment of change for me was during a major fundraising campaign for the library. I thought I was doing everything I could to get the best results, but the results were just not there. It was one of those scenarios where you are lost in your own fog. I could not see what I was missing. Fortunately, I was encouraged by one of my colleagues to join Toastmasters. With the feedback that I received; my passion was overpowering! I quickly learned that listening was as equally important as my passion. When you listen differently, you hear things that you might not have captured before. "Listening louder" allows a person to evaluate and better assess the information communicated, hence having enhanced communication with the individual or groups. Listening louder does not stop at just listening to the words or the tone of voice, that comes from your audience's mouth. Listen with your EYES too! What is their body doing? How does their face look? What are their hands doing? All that comes into play when you are listening louder. After all, fundraising and business relationships are all about meeting the needs of your donors or clients.

With a focus on enhanced listening, I started to see better results for our fundraising campaign - the fundraising bar on the thermometer kept rising, as did my energy and motivation. As my excitement increased so did my ability to

MAKE MORE WORK LESS by CONNECTING

connect better with the donors. In turn, the fundraising bar kept increasing higher and higher. I accredit learning enhanced listening skills as the turning point for me during the campaign. Not only did I learn about the needs of our donors, I also learned a lot more about the individuals, businesses and corporations that were offering to support our fundraising campaign. Prior to my learning how to listen, assess, and evaluate differently, I really believed that people would offer their support because we were running a fundraising campaign for a new library. I soon found out that it was more important as to WHY our potential donors would make an investment in literacy and the library.

Listening louder allowed me to better hear the needs of the donors and how THEIR needs would fit with our fundraising campaign. Were the businesses employing newcomers to Canada, or perhaps it was families or seniors that were long-time users of the library? What did our patrons and donors want? It was ALL about them! It wasn't just about the library's need to raise money. I had the opportunity to learn how much enhanced communication and leadership skills can achieve. Not just for myself, but also for our donors, our patrons, and all the people I engaged with in the community.

There have been several instances where youth that graduated from one of the communications and leadership programs that I facilitated, has come back to express their gratitude to me. Sharing their stories of success and how their lives have changed has added to WHY I do what I do. In turn, those stories and the lives that were changed become the reason future donors may donate to the library or another charitable organization.

The Magic of Connecting

Whether you are speaking to a large group of people or with an individual one-on-one, there comes a moment when you know that you have connected. When that occurs, something magical happens! Your message is delivered clearly and with passion and confidence, smiles can be seen, heads nod in approval AND you are having FUN!

Recently, I had the opportunity to be a keynote speaker for a conference hosted for Healthcare Aides. The topic was compassion. Hence, I built my keynote to include compassion for their patients, compassion for their colleagues, but most importantly, compassion for themselves. I felt it was a serious topic as Healthcare professionals can often experience compassion fatigue. During my keynote, I talked about practicing compassion in the many different aspects of our lives, how we should all laugh at ourselves more often. While speaking about the importance of laughter, I placed a red clown nose on my nose. This allowed me to laugh at myself, and the audience laughed with me. I provided each member of the audience with a small gift to help remind them to laugh at themselves more often. The gift was a bright red clown nose. My 'Ah-Ha' moment, where I knew that I had connected with my audience was at the end of the conference. What surprised me most was the number of people that lined up to have their picture taken with me. Of course, we all wore our bright red clown noses for the photos. I was overwhelmed with joy! I know that the Healthcare Aides truly got the message I delivered about compassion and about laughing at ourselves more often. It was a magical moment and one I shall not forget.

When that connection is made with the audience, the message remains. I hope that when the Healthcare Aides wear their clown noses or see a clown somewhere, they will be reminded about the importance of being a compassionate person and to laugh at themselves whenever they get the opportunity. You will be surprised what a kind gesture, a funny story, or your means of delivery can do. How you communicate your message can have a positive impact for your audience, and for some, your message can last a lifetime.

Emotional Connection

The most challenging aspects of fundraising is "selling" the potential donor on donating to the cause. Unlike selling a product or service, donating funds results with nothing physical going back to the donor. Sure, there may be a pin, a sticker, or some small promotional product associated with the campaign, but not an actual product that is equivalent to the amount of their donation. Therefore, connecting with the donor on an emotional level is vitally important.

In my previous story about the clown noses, I connected with the audience through laughter. An emotion, a feeling, one that will be remembered and triggered when they see a clown nose. At the very least, they will remember a happy feeling or a good thought. They may not remember the actual words that were spoken or the location of the conference, but they will remember how they felt. If we want to have a strong connection with our audience, there must be an emotional connection.

Many of my friends and colleagues have said to me: "*I don't know how you do it. I could never ask for money.*" Once

MAKE MORE WORK LESS by CONNECTING

again, the most important skill as a fundraiser, is passion for your cause. Equally, the fundraiser must meet the needs and the whys of the donor or prospective donors while effectively conveying the goal of the fundraising campaign. In almost every case, it is based on that emotional and heartfelt connection. You may be saying to yourself: *"How could a corporation have emotion?"* Well, in today's day and age, many of the large corporations are seeking professionals like engineers, project managers, accountants, and lawyers, people with various and diverse skills. Many of these professionals are volunteers or donate to various charitable organizations, and often times, they request the support of their employers. Businesses and corporations are made up of people, and it is those heartfelt connections that we speak to.

At the time, the cause that I was raising money for was the library and for literacy. Now, literacy is part of every profession and everything that we do. Every professional/individual in a business or corporation must have literacy to have been hired. When approaching individuals, professionals, businesses, and corporations, we focused on how literacy got them to where they are. What would it be like if an individual was illiterate? How would being illiterate affect their children or their relationships? What was it like when they first learned how to read? How did it feel when they got their first job or succeeded on a huge project? All those scenarios are tied to emotions and feelings.

We also realized that everyone's situation is different, and everyone's emotions are different. Whether you have the means to make a major donation of $10,000, $100,000, or $500,000, the emotions are no different than the emotions tied to those people donating $1, $5, or $20. I learned very quickly in our fundraising campaign for the library, that every dollar regardless of the amount, helped us to get closer to achieving our fundraising goal. I had many experiences where seniors would come and say they were so proud to donate their $5, $10, or $20. They just wanted to help us achieve our goal. When you connect emotionally with your donors, your audience or your client, you create a bond. The results of the bond can be from multiple outcomes but it all spawns from an emotional connection.

Nervous is GOOD?

One question that I get asked a lot is, "*What is your secret? How do you just go up on stage to speak to hundreds of people or walk into a corporate board room of people you've never met, and present a fundraising campaign?*" My answer usually surprises them. Something that I think about before a keynote address or a meeting with a donor or client is, "*I'm feeling nervous*". Colleagues and friends usually reply with: "*Well, how is that positive?*" My response, "*Being a little bit nervous keeps me on edge. It keeps me sharp. It keeps me humble.*" It also reminds me that, without donors or clients, I can't communicate. Reminding myself of that allows my communication to be real and authentic. The nerves also provide with me with a bit of excitement. You never know what can or will happen when presenting a keynote to an audience. One cannot prepare for everything; the projector or sound equipment may not work, more people than expected could show up, a celebrity might be in the audience. That little bit of the unknown is your nerves speaking and it can be exciting, hence, I make it fun every time I speak.

MAKE MORE WORK LESS by CONNECTING

Gratitude

Having raised funds for numerous nonprofit organizations, coached many individuals, and having spoken on many platforms, it can be very easy to get ahead of yourself. A reminder that every time you speak, every time you connect with someone, every time you are in a situation to deliver a message, it is an opportunity to make a difference. I appreciate every challenge, every opportunity, and everyone that I have met. Whether someone donated to a campaign or they were a member of an audience where I spoke, I look at this as a gift. Gratitude to each person that helps us to achieve our goals, is of utmost importance. Everyone wants to be valued and to be appreciated. People may or may not say it to you directly, but deep down, they know that you could not have achieved your goal without their support. Therefore, it's not only important to support yourself or your cause, but also to express appreciation and acknowledge the people who support you. Having people who motivate us and encourage us to achieve our goals, is indeed a gift to treasure. Never miss an opportunity to give a sincere THANK YOU to the people that support you, your business, or your charity. Appreciation can make someone's day, and even change a life.

Connecting Through the Community

It is because of all the lessons that I have learned from working within the community and raising funds for the community that I have been able to further develop my communication and leadership skills. In turn, I have applied passion and gratitude, listening louder, emotional connection, and my nerves to all aspects of my life. As a fundraiser, professional speaker, a coach and mentor, an

MAKE MORE WORK LESS by CONNECTING

entrepreneur, and a mom, enhanced communication skills and better connections with all the people in my life, have led me to stronger relationships, greater success and hope for a more compassionate tomorrow.

Chapter 6 – Community Connects

"Whatever words we utter should be chosen with care for people will hear them and be influenced by them for good or ill."

- Buddha -

Assurance Keys to Connecting

- Communication is in all aspects of our lives.
- We are all born to be leaders.
- Passion is the key.
- Listen Louder
- Connecting creates magic.
- Find the Why
- How can you appeal to them emotionally?
- Nerves equals excitement and fun.
- Gratitude and appreciation
- Create a compassionate tomorrow.

MAKE MORE WORK LESS by CONNECTING

Chapter - 7 -

Relationships Connects

By Dr. Ganz Ferrance

"After hearing about how important building relationships are in connecting, we figured that it would be a wise to talk to a psychologist who specializes in relationships. How can one Make More and Work Less by Connecting through relationships? When we connect, a bond is formed and the bond leads to a relationship. When that relationship is strong, the connection gets stronger, communication gets easier and things happen when you like the person you are dealing with and vice versa. Trust is ultimately built. To find out more about connecting and relationships, we chatted with The Positive Psychologist, a coach and author, Dr. Ganz Ferrance. He is a person who loves to share with his audience, his clients, and the people around him, how they can truly get the most mileage out of their lives."

MAKE MORE WORK LESS by CONNECTING

Effective Communication is Vital in Relationships

As a psychologist, I love figuring out how we work as people. I grew up in a family that was a little bit dysfunctional like most families are. When I was growing up, there were some things that weren't working in my family, things that weren't working in the way that I was running my life, and things that weren't working in my relationships. I thought to myself that I'd like to figure out how we work, how we think, what can make us better, so that we can have more success and that I can have more success. The more I looked into psychology, the more I found my passion in it. What drove me more was working with others and helping them make minor adjustments to change their lives. I get so happy seeing people tweak their lives and see how that plays out in big ways in their relationships, in their performance, in their success overall and their health and happiness. One common factor in a lot of relationship issues is communication. I have found that by making minor adjustments to our day-to-day communication habits, we can connect better with others which results in better relationships. Communication and relationships go hand in hand, you cannot have one without the other, and one will always affect the other.

There is no avoiding it. All relationships start with communication. Whether it is verbal, body, or written, communication is everywhere. Likewise, relationships are everywhere. If you have a strong relationship, then that generally means your communication is strong. If the relationship is weak then that means communication is sparse or ineffective. It works the same in all aspects of our lives -- at home, at work, at functions, and within ourselves. The success of a project at work generally stems from successful communications within the team. A poor performance of a sports team is usually because of poor communication among teammates and coaches. All of which are different forms and levels of relationships. Therefore, effective communication is vital in strong relationships.

Personal References

One form of effective communication is connecting through your personal experiences. We all go through life from different viewpoints and different perspectives. However, there are times where, what you go through and how you succeeded, relates directly to what someone else is experiencing. Being able to communicate your references effectively can be the turning point in someone else's life. There have been many occasions where I have reached into my personal experiences to connect with my clients with their situations. At the very least, it provides them with another perspective or support. I have found that when you share your personal experiences, you connect with your listener at another level, a level of trust, commonality, and or authenticity is established.

I published the book: *The Me Factor: Your Systematic Guide to Getting What the Hell You Want*, where the whole premise of the book stems from my own personal experiences. I have burnt myself out a couple times in my life trying to do everything I can do for the people around me, for my business, my clients, and my family. What I found was that as much as I tried, it was not working. I would push myself to work harder and I would do stuff that I believed was helping everyone, but it would not last. I would not have the energy to sustain it. What I did was I developed a system to keep me on track so that I would not burn myself out, I would have the energy, the skills, and everything I needed to give to the things or the people that were important to me. When I put the system together, what I found was, after a while, a lot of my clients were actually having the problems that I was dealing with and I saw that there were many commonalities. I realized that this is not just for me, it can be used for everybody as well. Once we understand how we function as people and what feeds us, then we can feed ourselves enough to be the high performers that we all deserve to be and be able to give more to the people around us that are important to us and increase our success. When we can connect with others through our personal experiences, we realize that we are not alone and that there or others out there that may have gone through what you are experiencing. That connection and that commonality strengthens the relationship.

Role Models

Becoming an effective communicator does not happen overnight. I was not always a good communicator. I pretty much sucked early in my life. A part of that was just what I saw around me. We are all products of our environment and if we do not have great role models or we are not conscious enough to go out and seek good role models, we basically just do what we grew up around; and that just seems normal to us. I did not see effective communication growing up and therefore, did not have the reference of a good, effective communicator. Knowing what I know now and looking around at other relationships, I realize that most people do not have good communication skills at all, mainly because they too do not have a good effective communicator as a role model. They do their best and muddle through life, but they do not know all the intricacies and all the little pieces that can make a huge difference in their lives.

When I realized after several bad relationships that something was not right, I got some help. I found a mentor, a coach in communication. I started seeing a psychologist for myself, and started learning how, not just from an academic sense how we work, but also from a personal sense how we work. I started working on my communication skills as a person and my relationships improved. I learned how to listen more actively, I learned how to use the right speech patterns that get heard. The biggest thing I learned, was to develop the patience to understand; that I was able to slow down enough to be able to hear what the other person is saying and really understand them before I try to fix a problem or come up with the solutions for whatever the situation is. Surrounding yourself with those who you want to learn from or emulate, will get you closer to what you want to become. Your role models will show you the way, your coaches will challenge, support, and teach you. And eventually, you too will become the role model.

Light Bulb On!

When you communicate effectively, you connect with your audience or your partner and when that happens, a light bulb turns on. When I first started doing therapy and was working with clients, couples especially, but even the one-on-one clients, there were times when I saw the light bulb turn on and I saw people light up. I saw them start to communicate better, I saw them show more compassion toward each other. It was like a different person when a connection is made. When you see that love come across between people, who have been fighting for a while, and some understanding dawned, it's a gratifying feeling. That is when I know I got

MAKE MORE WORK LESS by CONNECTING

through to them, when that light bulb in their minds turn on, and you know it will not be forgotten.

I remember running one of my Me Factor workshops, and one of the participants stood out. We were going through the system and part of the system is a decision-making process that we do. It has numbers in it, and it evaluates all the different factors of your life to make sure you're keeping everything in balance so that you are not going to make a decision that is lopsided. Part way through this process, the participant looked up and shouted, "*I know what I need to do!*" We were looking at current job situations, what they were not happy about with that job, versus looking at another job. After he shouted, "*I know what I need to do!*" he left and went to an interview. Later that day he e-mailed me and said:

"Thank you so much for doing the exercise with me because it helped clarify what I wanted. I was kicking the idea of quitting my job around for months in my mind. After we connected, I went to the interview, took the job right there and quit the other job that afternoon."

That was one of those times where it was a pointed moment where it felt like OK, yeah, the message got across to him. Getting the message across to others has everything to do with connecting at a trust level, and to do so, one must listen and watch carefully to assess the next step or next set of words.

Controlling your Anxiety

On many occasions, I have been asked what one key factor is, in communicating effectively. I work with many individuals of all different personalities, egos, backgrounds, and ethnicities, and there are times when conversations get

MAKE MORE WORK LESS by CONNECTING

complicated and become challenging to connect. At times like that, I think back to one of my mentors.

I had a good teacher when I was in graduate school and one of the lines stuck with me. This works for psychologists, business people, salespeople, people in relationships, and everyone who needs to communicate.

> *"My No. 1 responsibility is controlling my own anxiety."*

That is the No. 1 thing. When I control my own anxiety and stay grounded and stay present, it is much easier to hear what the other person is saying. If you are in a sales situation, you hear the objections or see what kind of feedback you're getting from the person's body language. In my job, working with a couple or a family who is in distress or who is having a very difficult time, when I can manage my own anxiety and stay calm, my calmness, that sense of rootedness, helps the other people feel safe. It helps them to feel that, if I am OK, then they will probably be OK too. That brings down the stress in the whole room and helps me to hear them better. They are much more open to any kind of feedback or any kind of interventions that I might suggest at that point. As I mentioned before, once you can hear, you can connect.

Connecting with Relationships

Working with many individuals and groups as a psychologist, has really emphasized how important effective communication is in building relationships. It is those very relationships that makes everything go smooth at your home, your business, and in your job. Therefore, it is obvious that if one wants to succeed in anything that they do, whether it is in business, sports, parenting, etc. one must see the value in

MAKE MORE WORK LESS by CONNECTING

strong relationships, which all begins with effective communication and connecting. Developing those great communications skills will definitely show that you have the ME Factor.

As an appreciation for all those who have reached this point of the book, I would like to offer you a FREE audio download of my book, "The Me Factor", go to: https://askdrganz.com/pages/giveaway

MAKE MORE WORK LESS by CONNECTING

MAKE MORE WORK LESS by CONNECTING

Chapter 7 – Relationships Connects

"If you have an important point to make, don't try to be subtle or clever. Use a pile driver. Hit the point once. Then come back and hit it again. Then hit it a third time - a tremendous whack."

- Winston Churchill -

Assurance Keys to Connecting

- There is a direct correlation between effective communication and relationships.

- Personal references build trust, commonality, and authenticity.

- Personal stories show that you are not alone.

- Role Models / Coaches / Mentors play a great role in how you communicate and connect with others.

- When you connect, you turn their inner light bulb-ON!

- Control your own anxiety.

MAKE MORE WORK LESS by CONNECTING

Chapter - 8 -
Sales/Marketing Connects

By Stacy Richter

"Relationships are key to all communication, and for sales and marketing, it is about building relationships. The better you can build relationships, the more effective your sales and your marketing materials are. Not only will you increase your sales, but also your clients will continue to come back. When you connect with your clientele and understand how companies and brands reach out to their consumers, it is obvious that connecting through sales and marketing is vital to the success of a business. To dig deeper into connecting through sales and marketing, we picked the brain of Stacy Richter, The Marketing Mindbender! He is a person who is able to generate leads and convert with his copy writing, sales strategies, and marketing creativity!"

MAKE MORE WORK LESS by CONNECTING

MAKE MORE WORK LESS by CONNECTING

Sales and Marketing is Communication!

Marketing and sales penetrate every part of our lives. We experience it every day for as long as we live. When you think about marketing and sales in general, they are all about the communication. There is not a single moment in our lives, sleeping or awake, that we are not impacted through sales and marketing. We're either receiving messages or sending them. These messages come from (or are delivered to) your friends, family, advertisers, radio, media, and online. We are communicating one way or another. That's what is super exciting about sales and marketing. One person can potentially have an impact on hundreds of thousands of lives every day.

Marketing and sales require two or more people. Marketing and sales do not travel one way. They are a two-way channel between people, not things. This is how our world gets interconnected. When we're talking about communication within marketing and sales, it's always between people, for people, and by people.

Ongoing Process

Understanding your clients, partners, and audience stems from effective communication. You must first build relationships to grasp what people want, how people feel and how they will react. Building relationships is a never-ending process and you will never know it all, although you can become a more effective communicator. Developing your communication skills is continuous because it enables building relationships with new and old audiences. The moment you think you "know" it all, is the moment you are in trouble.

MAKE MORE WORK LESS by CONNECTING

Communication is one of those things where you can always improve. You are always reaching different people for different reasons. Every time I am speaking on stage, pitching a proposal in a boardroom, or doing interviews on camera, I am always thinking "*Is there a different way of doing this? How can I do it better?*"

The first hint I got when I learned that, I really needed to improve my communication skills, was in my first-year university. My confidence was high because I had a couple of years of adult life and was about to embark on my university career. The assignment was to write a position paper about a topic of my choosing. To say the least, the paper I turned in was awful. The grade was terrible. There were spelling and grammatical mistakes all over it. When I reread the paper, I realized how bad my communication was. Communication includes verbal and written. Seeing that grade and feeling the embarrassment was the kick in the pants that I needed. It was at that moment that I promised myself that going forward, I needed to make sure that no matter what I do, every message must always be:

Well Prepared   *Well Practiced*

Thoughtfully Crafted   *Persuasive*

Understandable

Get Noticed with Effective Communication

When you communicate effectively, many new doors and opportunities open up for you. Whether it is in business, with family, with friends, or at work. What is also astonishing is how one opportunity paves the way to another and another. It becomes exponential!

This was evident during my time in public relations. Public relations is a very heavy print and written style of communication. Thankfully, I had mastered my craft because I wrote that horrible essay back in university.

Securing a client is step No. 1. I recall working with one particular client. During the interview process, we had to communicate effectively with him. Understanding what he wanted and presenting him strategies that will solve his problems was the core of our messaging. We were listening to his concerns and vision.

When that was understood, we were able to create and propose the right strategies for that client. Our client was a very wealthy, astute business individual who owned several successful businesses already. We were presenting him a PR (public relations) strategy that would get one of his companies more visibility in its market. After successfully securing this client, we moved on to the next step, putting the strategy into action.

We had to convince relevant media outlets to feature the story we put together for our client. Therefore, not only did we have to sell the message and strategy to the owner of the business (our client), but we also had to sell it to the targeted media outlets. Understanding how each outlet operates, what its audiences like or dislike, how to add value to the

MAKE MORE WORK LESS by CONNECTING

media and their readers, enabled us to get our client's story out to a wide range of outlets and readers.

We were able to secure that particular client over a half million dollars in ad equivalency for the retainer they paid us (a return of over 13 times) through PR and media. The coverage included cover pages on trade magazines and 10-page full color features in several different magazines across Canada and the United States. All of that exposure for our client, and the success of our business, was the result of effective communication!

Words to Remember

Not all partnerships and results have happy endings like the one I shared earlier. In marketing and sales, you need to work with many different people, with different backgrounds, and different motives. You will encounter campaigns that fail, clients who are difficult, or audiences that give you a hard time.

At times like that, it is always tough because you rarely know until it's too late. It's after the fact that we learn what we could have done differently to communicate more effectively. It is our learnings from those situations that we bring forward, reflect on them, and make adjustments in the future. I always remind myself every time we go to write a piece, do a video, get a graphic, write an advertisement, or speak to my friends and family, that communication is a 360-degree channel. This is the one thing that I will always remember.

"What part of whose mind do you want to occupy? Then what do you want them to do, when you're there?"

If you can figure that part out, then the numbers game starts to play a little bit more in your favour. The tough deals, the tough clients, and the tough negotiations become just a little easier. As you keep that in mind and gain more experience, the easier deals seem to come a little faster. Everything just improves. Even if it is only a few small steps at a time.

Preparation

Mindset is vital for communicating effectively. Especially in marketing and sales! Before you walk into a boardroom, go up on stage, or meet with a big client, consider how you set your mind. It can be the difference between failure or success, contract or no contract, magazine coverage or television special.

For me, there is no secret. Effective communication happens long before that moment that you jump on stage or get in front of that investor. It all depends on your level of preparation.

Recently, I had a chance to present my fintech company in front of a room of 150 very astute, wealthy executives, and I had three minutes. I started preparing that three-minute presentation three weeks before the event and probably spent close to 40 hours on a three-minute presentation. Right before the moment I was about to take that stage, the one thing that went through my mind was *"This is going to be great!"*. I reminded myself *"What part of whose mind do I want to occupy?"* It was the preparation leading up to that point that gave me the confidence on stage.

Preparation is the key. Preparation allows you to envision:
- What will happen?
- What questions could be asked?

MAKE MORE WORK LESS by CONNECTING

- How you could feel?
- Who might be there?
- Who is listening?

You can prepare for all these. When you are significantly prepared, you will not be surprised or be caught off guard. Even if something does happen that you do not expect, the preparation enables you to address the circumstances in a calm and effective manner. However long you need to prepare leading up to that moment is the secret. And that is NOT a secret!

Communication is Everywhere!

Effective communication not only affects your sales and marketing results, it affects all aspects of your life. The moment you talk or look at a printed word, you are communicating.

Everybody needs to figure out how they're communicating. Is your way of communicating working? Are you getting the results that you want? Regardless, we will all benefit from improving our communication. We can never know it all.

People who think that they do not need to work on their communication skills because of the type of work they do or their personality type are people who have a preset mindset about communication. They need to look at communication from another perspective. What would happen if they did have better communication? How can effective communication change their lives?

We are always trying to persuade someone else of something. The moment you need someone else's outside influence, you need to communicate. It might be at your job.

MAKE MORE WORK LESS by CONNECTING

You may need to convince your supervisor or your manager to approve a budget. You may need them to approve your vacation. You need to figure out how to communicate effectively. We are all doing sales and marketing whether you like it or not.

It extends outside the workplace as well. You may be communicating with your spouse. You may be communicating with your children, who are the best negotiators I've ever seen! They never take 'No' for an answer! You know exactly where they sit every single time on every single issue.

We are always communicating regardless of your background, career, and age. Take a look at another perspective anytime you want somebody to do something you want. Effective communication is getting them to do that thing YOU want for THEIR reasons.

As a thank you to all the readers who have gotten this far, I have included 5 BIG bonuses to help you on your way in marketing and sales. Simply download the gifts at:

https://www.marketingmindbender.com/make-more-work-less-bonuses

MAKE MORE WORK LESS by CONNECTING

	Item	Description
Bonus #1	Lifetime registration for the Marketing Mindbender Platform	The #1 platform for local business marketing. Grow your business with access to on-demand marketing services. The Marketing Mindbender is the 21st century approach to successful local business marketing
Bonus #2	Unlimited use of the Advertising Intelligence App.	Live digital ad reporting and analysis. Advertising Intelligence brings your business' ad campaigns under one roof so you can see what's working across various platforms. Uncover recipes behind rockstar campaigns, pinpoint what's making your business money, and use automation to stay on top of reporting.
Bonus #3	Unlimited access to the Listing Builder App	Kick-start your online presence! Listing Builder empowers your business to start the conversation about digital solutions with local customers.
Bonus #4	Lifetime access to the Marketing Mindbender VIP Lounge	Exclusive and Private VIP Lounge in Facebook. Mingle with other high level Marketing Mindbender members and special guests. Chat and network about marketing your business with successful entrepreneurs.
Bonus #5	Lifetime access to the Beginners Guide to Facebook Ads	This is the next best thing to having an expert on the subject, right beside you, showing you how it's done. Access to 12 modules of video instruction, supporting materials and ongoing support.

Chapter 8 – Sales/Marketing Connects

"Electric communication will never be a substitute for the face of someone who with their soul encourages another person to be brave and true."

- Charles Dickens -

Assurance Keys to Connecting

- Marketing and sales are a two-way channel between people, for people, and by people.

- Communication is a never ending process.

- Is your message: well-prepared, well-practiced, thoughtfully crafted, persuasive, and understandable?

- Results of effective communication is exponential.

- "What part of whose mind do you want to occupy. Then what do you want them to do, when you're there?"

- Communicate something you want for their reasons.

- Communication is a pathway to relationships.

MAKE MORE WORK LESS by CONNECTING

Chapter - 9 -

Investing Connects

By Shin Kawaguchi

"After seeing how marketing and sales are a form of communication, we figured that if one wanted to be successful in investing, then communication must be important as well. We went through our contacts and found an investor like no other. Not only is he an investor, but he is also an engineer, an insurance broker, a real estate agent, an online salesperson, a coach, and a birther! With all his experiences and roles, he has excelled in every single one! So, there was no doubt that we had to seek out Shin Kawaguchi and see how effective communication assisted him in his ventures, his roles, and him as an investor."

MAKE MORE WORK LESS by CONNECTING

Communication is Vital in Investing!

When you are an investor or a person who is always looking for opportunities to invest, being able to communicate effectively is vital. What is so exciting and motivating about being an investor is that every day is a little bit different, there are no two investments that are identical. That also means there is no conversation or communication that is the same. Every day keeps you on your toes. Every day is an opportunity, and every day effective communication is vital to the outcomes of deals, opportunities, and conversations. We did a lot of real estate, which is what introduced us to the investing world. Once again, every single real estate deal has its own little twists and turns to it. Each deal had its own unique conversation, negotiation, and persuasion technique. Whether you are successful in a negotiation or in persuading someone, has everything to do with your effectiveness in communicating. So, it's never a boring job. You always have to think on your feet, you have to think quickly, and you have to be ready for anything. Communicating effectively is no different than effective problem-solving, which is a big part in investing.

Continuous Learning

One of the most important traits as an investor is the mindset of continuous learning. When you have an interest in learning and acquiring knowledge, life is never boring. That is why my wife and I are involved in so many different industries and roles from real estate to engineering to insurance to being a birther! All of that requires a forever learning attitude. Effective communication has had a major impact in all the roles that I have had. Due to that mindset of continuous learning, I am eager to improve my skills every day as an

MAKE MORE WORK LESS by CONNECTING

investor and communicator. The more effective of a communicator I become, the more successful I am.

I am venturing into online marketing, which happens to be one area I struggled with. Well, guess what? One of the elements of online marketing is starting a YouTube channel, which means learning to speak online and make videos! Again, it's all about effective communication. It's everywhere and there is always something to learn and improve on.

No One Is Born With it

People are not born effective communicators. No matter how successful an investor is or how famous a speaker is, you can ask them how they felt the first time they spoke in front of a crowd of people. You will likely hear the same story over and over again. How they were scared, nervous, and how they wanted to run away. Even to this day, the best of them will be a little bit nervous when speaking in front of a large group. The key is harnessing those nerves and using it to your advantage. All of it was learned through process and practice. Even now I'm still trying to improve on my speaking and communicating.

There are two main elements of communicating that I have found to make all communication more effective:

1) Direct your audience to the message you are delivering.

2) A call to action.

MAKE MORE WORK LESS by CONNECTING

Directing the Audience to your Message

When you are able to guide your audience toward the message you are delivering, it makes it a lot easier for them to follow and understand it. Ask questions and tell stories that the audience can relate to and answer themselves, allow them to go searching for the message on their own. When the audience is able to figure out where you are leading them, they will understand it more because they *"discovered"* it on their own.

Think back to when you were a child or when you are teaching your child math or science. When they ask you a question or when you asked a question, did you give your child the answer right away? Did the teacher give you the answer right away? Most likely the teacher or you would have asked more questions so that you or your child would answer each question so that eventually it will lead you or your child to the final answer. Guiding you or your child to the answer on their own allows them or you to retain the information longer and also understand the answer better. Having that ability to guide is the first key to communicating effectively.

Call to Action

When all is said and done there is always a purpose or an action point at the end. You can say whatever you want but unless people are actually doing something, your message usually gets lost. Especially in sales, at the very end of your communication, speech or pitch, whatever you want to tell somebody, give him or her something to do, give them an e-mail and say *"Call me for more information,"* or sell him or her your product or ask him or her for the sale. You have to do something at the end. Otherwise, people just forget about you quickly.

MAKE MORE WORK LESS by CONNECTING

Giving a call to action is no different than that teacher giving you homework after you "*discovered*" the answer. To cement it in your memory, taking the action of doing practice problems in the homework, gives you the opportunity to exercise that new found knowledge. As a leader or an investor, if you are trying to get something from your people, you can give the best motivational speech you ever gave, but if you do not give them something to do with it at the end, it is forgotten.

Therefore, no matter what your message is, once you have guided them to it, give them a question, an exercise, or a course of action, so that they can have your message in their mind and give it more thought. The stronger your call to action is, the longer you stay in their memory, and the longer you stay in their mind, the more effective of a communicator you are.

Mindset Shift

Once you are able to guide your audience to the message and give a strong call to action, there is always that moment when you realize that they've got it. I can think of a few times, while I was coaching my investing clients when I witnessed someone's mindset shift. It is a very interesting and a cool moment when they're realizing something within themselves. In this particular case, the clients started off doubting themselves, doubting their ability, and asking if real estate investing was for them, to the point where they were saying: "*Yeah, I can actually do this!*". You see their whole demeanor change as they realize that it's not really a hard skillset to learn. It's just a mindset thing. Lots of people's mindset changes when you effectively communicate to them your message. They can move on with that. They put that "*Can't*

Do It" attitude behind them and move toward something new. That's what I think the first step to succeeding is.

Secret Weapon

Effective communication not only allows you to motivate others and help them realize what they are capable of, but it can also become your secret weapon for navigating through difficult scenarios, and as an investor, these scenarios occur a lot. From working with tenants to negotiating complex deals, there will always be individuals who do not see things eye to eye with you. Emotions are usually brought into the conversation and egos start getting in the way. It is human nature to get defensive and fight for what you want, and when both parties are doing the same thing, that is when things get out of hand. When you communicate effectively, you need to be the side that is calm and do your best to keep the emotions out of the conversation. Understand where the other party is coming from and see why he or she is asking or reacting that way. What you want to do is to build trust.

A lot of it comes down to trust, always operate in the model of *"Trust but Verify"* and be willing to give people a chance. In the world of investing, the first time you meet others, people always put their best foot forward and it's not really until you encounter adversity that you see the true side of them. That's when you have to communicate effectively and seek understanding. Sometimes, it comes down to what kind of feelings you get from the person. Is it someone you can trust? Are you asking the right questions to give you the right feelings? Are you guiding them to the outcome that you seek? All that means communicating effectively.

MAKE MORE WORK LESS by CONNECTING

Shake Shake Shake!

As an investor, it is vital to be in the right frame of mind and also have the right energy when walking into a boardroom or meeting that potential partner or investor. Your first impression sets up the entire meeting. Therefore, it's good to go in with lots of energy. You have to be a step above everyone else's energy in the crowd. That is key. When you have the mindset of, *"I'm ready to GO!"*, the audience feels that in the first five seconds of meeting you. As soon as you get on the stage, the audience will feel the energy from you. Your whole speech can change paths just based on that. Your audience becomes more susceptible and engaged. You will find that the members are easier to guide and more willing to follow your call to action. Your first step, your first word, your first facial expression is what sets you up for success! That all starts with your mindset.

Whatever you need to do to pump yourself up, do it before you go on stage. You can do a clap. You can do a cheer. Just get ready and loosened up a little bit. Watch what athletes do right before a game or a big race. They listen to music. They do a chant. They huddle. They jump up and down. They get pumped and ready to go! That is no different than what we should all be doing right before we go to speak or go into a huge meeting. For myself, I like a little shoulder shaking and a little clap. Just the act of clapping and moving, the act of moving gets me pumped up and ready to go!

You want Growth? Communicate Effectively

There is no avoiding effective communication if you want to grow. As an investor and someone who has been in many different roles and industries, everywhere I turn I need to communicate effectively to succeed. Every new skill or

MAKE MORE WORK LESS by CONNECTING

industry that I learn requires communication, and the better the communication, the faster I become at learning or succeeding in it.

The power of persuasion will get you anywhere. If you had one skill that you could master to be successful, it is to be good at persuasion, and persuasion is effective communication. If you can get other people to follow you, to believe in you, to understand you, to buy into what you're doing, the world's your oyster.

The world is changing so fast and new opportunities come up all the time. One thing that does not change is the need to communicate. The world of online business is taking over as you see retail stores shutting down. Everything is moving towards online. Regardless communication is the key. In fact, with so much being online, being able to communicate effectively is even more important as there is more competition. If you are looking at starting a business or being an investor, you need to build an online presence, you need to communicate in a way where you stand out above all the others. Learn about marketing, learn about online sales and learn about getting noticed. All of which are effective communication.

MAKE MORE WORK LESS by CONNECTING

Chapter 9 – Investing Connects

"If you invest the time earlier to create structure and process around communication, planning and goal-setting, you can prevent missteps before they occur."

- Christine Tsai -

Assurance Keys to Connecting

- No conversation or communication is the same.

- Communicating effectively is no different than effective problem-solving.

- There is always something to learn and improve on.

- Two elements of effective communication:
    - Direct your audience to the message you are delivering.
    - A call to action.

- Mindset shifts when message gets through.

- Trust but verify.

- Ask questions to lead your audience to the grand answer.

- Get ready; get pumped up; shake; and let loose.

- World is changing fast, but communication is still vital.

MAKE MORE WORK LESS by CONNECTING

MAKE MORE WORK LESS by CONNECTING

Chapter - 10 -
Entrepreneurship Connects
By Chan Kawaguchi

"Having a discussion with Shin was enlightening and astonishing. It is very interesting how effective communication impacts the ability to invest successfully! Seeing how Shin was involved with so many different industries and how communicating effectively had an impact on each one, another individual came to mind. Someone who has a completely different personality than Shin but was also involved in many industries. From being a paralegal, to an insurance sale team manager, to a file clerk, to online businesses, and a mother, she completes the power couple – Chan Kawaguchi. Chan has utilized effective communication throughout all her roles, which created momentum and motivation to become an Entrepreneur Disruptor!"

MAKE MORE WORK LESS by CONNECTING

MAKE MORE WORK LESS by CONNECTING

Mindset of an Entrepreneur

As an entrepreneur, one thing that we all have in common is that we have the mindset of always improving ourselves. We look for challenges that will sharpen our skills. We surround ourselves with people who push us to be better. We seek opportunities that will expand our knowledge. Once we are confident in something, we tend to look for the next thing that will excite us again and again.

Hard work is not an issue as long as I am constantly growing, even if it meant taking lesser roles. From office admin to becoming a paralegal, then back to a file clerk but with greater upside. I saw opportunities, I acted on them, and proved that someone without a degree or certification can do more than just a competent job. I still went into work with a smile on my face and felt privileged like it was really the best job around - and it was! People in the company noticed, and they moved me up the corporate ladder pretty fast. In about a couple months, I took a position in the accounting department. From there, my husband and I took on real estate investing, going to training sessions and hiring a coach. Within eight months of implementing what we learned, we did more than 15 real estate transactions with calculated risk and multiple exit strategies. I kept on learning and expanding to other businesses, to insurance, to online platforms, etc. Every step of the journey, being able to communicate effectively goes a long way. Just the simple gesture of putting a smile on your face every day communicates a positive feeling to those around you. Combine that with the way we say things, the way we move, and the words we use, have allowed us to succeed in all our ventures. Effective communication gives you results and with more and more results you get momentum.

MAKE MORE WORK LESS by CONNECTING

For communicating effectively, one of the most powerful strategies is telling a story. It can be your journey to becoming who you currently are, your back story/history, or stories of others becoming successful. As you pursue new challenges, there is going to be hiccups along the way, mistakes and failures, but do not stop. This journey creates a back story, which is way more powerful than the transformation of: "Look at me now. This is all that I've accomplished and the money I made". Without a back story, it is "selling." When you share a story, you share a personal bond. When I had the opportunity to work in the insurance industry, I knew nothing about insurance and outside sales, but with a keen sense of learning and action-taking, I found a way to become effective and good at it. I told a lot of my back stories to everyone I could and helped solve their problems. I was literally changing people's beliefs (false beliefs they had, whether it was in real estate investing, cryptocurrencies, insurance, etc.), by telling stories. A lot of the times, my clients and customers want to hear my back story, because it is relatable and genuine.

To communicate effectively as an entrepreneur, you must be a problem solver. Always ask yourself, how can I help solve their problem, and how do I add value first before promoting anything. That is where listening and observing becomes vital. When you listen and observe effectively, you can communicate and solve problems and add value effectively.

How to Talk and Listen

One can never finish learning how to communicate effectively. I am still working on being an effective communicator. Even when it comes to communicating with my husband and children. Whether it is family or a business

MAKE MORE WORK LESS by CONNECTING

partner or a potential client, to get what you want, you cannot just tell them to do something. When I realized that the way I was communicating was not getting through to them, I researched and looked for solutions. The interesting thing is, one of the most helpful resources was a children's book call "*How to Talk so Your Kids Will Listen and How to Listen so Your Kids Will Talk.*" The keys of this book can be applied to all scenarios of your life, whether it is relationships, businesses, or investing.

The secret to communicating is understanding that communication is a relationship. For the communication to be effective, we must want to ensure that everyone involved in the conversation is receiving what he or she wants. When everyone gets what he or she wants within the reasonable limits, then there is a symbiotic relationship, symbiotic communication. You can create a blueprint as to what you need to focus on during a conversation:

1. Listen
2. What are they saying?
3. Paraphrase
4. How can you help with that?
5. How can you add value?
6. Give a relatable personal story.
7. Ask questions to reaffirm what they want.
8. Ask questions to help them get to a common solution.
9. Make your suggestion.

Recently, I had a conversation with a friend of mine. She was complaining about how her kids would not eat their vegetables. I too had this same issue with my kids. I listened to the issue and I understood that the end goal was to get her

MAKE MORE WORK LESS by CONNECTING

kids to eat vegetables. I had a solution, and I knew how to add value to her. However, before I gave her my solution, I shared my own story about how I found a solution, and how I got my kids to eat vegetables. I began telling her about smoothie recipes that I was trying out and that it was so good that I gave it to my kids who also enjoyed them. These smoothies were so packed full of fruits, spinach and greens that I could replace our meals. So not only were my kids getting their vegetables, we also made it a fun part of our day making smoothies together. My friend was so excited and wanted to implement it right away with her kids, which she did.

Now imagine if all I said after she complained that her kids did not eat vegetables was: "*Go buy an $800 Vitamix.*" She would have said I was crazy! It is because I was able to communicate with my own story, listen to what she really wanted, and added value that she didn't need to be "sold' on getting a Vitamix.

Who Are You Working With?

Everyone has his or her own way of doing things and thinking about things. Therefore, you cannot expect that how you communicate will be effective with everyone. Understanding the personality of the person you are communicating with allows you to adapt and customize the way you communicate, so that you can get the most from them.

When I was in the insurance industry, I took on a role where I had to manage a team of sales agents. Managing people was not something I thoroughly enjoyed doing. I started losing my passion of being in the insurance industry. My biggest problem was that my message didn't get through to

MAKE MORE WORK LESS by CONNECTING

everyone. It felt like I had to repeat myself all the time and needed to handhold certain individuals that did not seem to want to buy into the culture that I wanted to create. I finally realized that the issue was me. I was not communicating the right way. I expected everyone to know what I was saying and know my belief systems. But how is that possible when they are NOT me?

What helped me was knowing what personality my team members were for me to communicate my message effectively to them. This was a technique that I learned from my Oil and Gas years. It was standard procedure for the company to make you take a test to discover what type of personality you are of four types. Each individual had to post their personality type on their door. For example, I am a focused and very detailed orientated person. It was befitting for my role in the accounting department. What that would mean to a teammate who was a different personality type than mine, say those who do not like details and have an eye for the bigger picture, is that for them to communicate effectively to me and to get what they wanted from me, they would need to understand who they were working with. For example, I do not like surprises. I like to be well-prepared in advance. Therefore, if you were to spring up to my office with an impromptu meeting without any notice in advance, I would not be sold in what you were trying to get me to do. Now had you e-mailed me a list of tasks and an agenda, have a call to action and let me know in advance that we were going to have this meeting, I would be more inclined to help you.

To communicate what I wanted my team to do effectively, I realized that I needed to communicate it in a way that was befitting to their personality, not mine. Whether I needed more visuals, more step-by-step instructions, more examples, or a combination of all the above, to be effective I needed to understand how others receive information best.

Items to Keep in Mind

Every time I go to an investor meeting, a business meeting or speak on stage, I have six things that I always keep in mind. As long as I can hit each of the six things, I can be confident that some members of the audience will do what I want them to do, but at the very least I know that I will be remembered.

1) Ask Questions
2) Have them say YES
3) Keep it Simple
4) Tell My Story
5) Share my Epiphany
6) Give them a Call to Action

When I sit down with potential insurance clients, I ask questions that relate to them. Something that I notice on my way there. You will find that being observant is very advantageous. For instance, "*I noticed you have small bicycles on the driveway. Do you have children?*" Each question is crafted so that it is taking inventory for me to help them solve their problem. I then share my own story or other borrowed stories relating to kids and then sharing my own epiphany. The potential client will then come to their own realization and understanding. That is when you can offer a call to action. This format can be applied to all of life's scenarios. Whether it is with your wife, husband, kids, business partner, investor, coaching client, or a customer, it is a format that allows you to communicate effectively what you want at the same time getting them what they want.

MAKE MORE WORK LESS by CONNECTING

A simple way to remember this is with the acronym:

U.P.S.N.O.

Unaware (unaware of the problem)
Product Aware
Service Aware
Niche Aware
Offer Aware

When individuals are unaware of a problem or situation, they become confused. Therefore, you must educate them before you offer a solution. This is where your stories and questions come into play. After they understand the scenario, now you can offer advice, solutions and tips, and present your offer, call to action or a take away. If you have done all the above, then you have effectively communicated your message.

Communication Affects Everyone and the Future

Throughout my journey of entrepreneurship from industry to industry, there has not been a role or scenario or position where being able to communicate effectively did not have a positive impact on the results. Whether I was a file clerk, an accountant, a sales team manager, and now an online marketer, communication is vital in each area.

Most people in the insurance industry, literally put themselves in a sales position. For marketing, it is the act of changing people's beliefs through stories. An engineer who does calculations all day needs to communicate their findings to the client or supervisor. A janitor will need to ensure that a potential issue is communicated to owners or trades so that

MAKE MORE WORK LESS by CONNECTING

the right course of action is taken. You will find that no matter the role, the better you communicate, the more opportunities you get, the more results you have, and the more people want to work with you. That may lead to promotions, new opportunities, and/or relationships. Some people use the stage to communicate their message. Some people do it through writing books and courses; and some do it through online sales funnels. You will find that when you communicate effectively you gain two very important elements:

You will have better **TIME** and **ENERGY** management.

The world is becoming more technologically based and everyone has something to say and share. When you can effectively get your message across to others, you will save on time and energy. Therefore, effective communication is getting more and more important as we advance in our lives. If we have a message, service, or product, we need to ask how we can get our message out there quickly to more people. However, with this digital era, it is unfortunate that our attention span is only seconds. So how we communicate and market our message must grab the audience's attention very quickly. That is where entrepreneurs must be creative, full of momentum, and always improving.

Chapter 10 – Entrepreneurship Connects

"Miscommunication is the No. 1 cause of all problems; communication is your bridge to other people. Without it, there's nothing. So, when it's damaged, you have to solve all these problems it creates."

- Earl Sweatshirt -

Assurance Keys to Connecting

- Share your back story and journey.

- Communication leads to results to momentum to opportunity.

- Effective communication is effective problem-solving.

- Communication is a relationship.

- Understand the personality of your audience to get your message across.

- Be observant of your surroundings to give you inventory of how to add value.

- Effective communication is time and energy management.

MAKE MORE WORK LESS by CONNECTING

Chapter - 11 -
Coaching Connects

MAKE MORE WORK LESS by CONNECTING

MAKE MORE WORK LESS by CONNECTING

New yet... Tested, Proven, and True

Let me know if this sounds familiar. You were given a task to complete. You knew that completing this task will set you apart from others, and at the same time, challenge yourself to grow into a better leader. The great part of this task is that you will be sent to a course, to a destination that you always wanted to visit on the company's budget to attend a conference on the newest innovations in your industry. The catch is that when you are back, you are to do a presentation to your colleagues, your superiors, and the upper management of the company on what you have learned. You have had no experience speaking to large groups of people and were given no prior training. Has something like this happened to you before? Or something similar? Like a group project in school, emcee an event, or your very first speech in a Toastmasters Club? Would it not have been nice to have someone hold your hand "figuratively" throughout the process, guide you with the preparation, and advise you on what works or what does not work? How I wish I had someone who would have supported me during my first presentation at my workplace or even my first speech in Toastmasters. I was nervous, shaky, and probably very boring! That is where a coach would have been very helpful.

The concept of coaching has been around for ages. From the beginning of time when a father took his son hunting for the first time to the blacksmith's apprentice learning the trade. Even today, a lot of coaching is happening in front of our eyes, yet many people do not recognize how important a coach is in everyone's life. Chances are great, you have a coach that you can think of right now. Whether it is your mother, your father, your hockey coach or your best friend, everyone can coach, and everyone is being coached.

MAKE MORE WORK LESS by CONNECTING

What is very interesting is that for sports and athletes, having a coach is common sense. When you watch gymnastics or figure skating you always see the athletes' coaches supporting them, encouraging them and giving them pointers in areas that need improvement. This mentality however is not the same when we talk about enhancing our speaking skills to be more effective. At the same time, for one to be an effective coach, the coach also needs to be an effective communicator and connect with who he or she is coaching.

Having knowledge and resources is one thing. Being able to put all the pieces together is another. That is where a coach comes into play, and it is the role of the coach to be able to communicate that to the individual. Coaches are able to take a look at what your situation is and assist you with what to do and also with what is needed to reach your goals.

Over the years, we have gone from being coached (still being coached), to coaching clients ourselves. As mentioned previously in this book, the most effective way of learning is to teach others. With the support from our own coaches, we have been able to apply their skills and methods in our coaching while at the same time adjust and learn how to coach effectively by coaching others. Having coached many individuals, whether in speaking, real estate, investing or business, we have found that the better we connect with the client the more successes and results the client will achieve.

The biggest challenge as a coach is that the product of coaching are the results. It is the value that is perceived by the individual being coached. The amount of time being coached does not necessarily mean the amount of results the student will achieve. As we see in sports on many occasions, coaches can coach teams for years without winning a championship. Yet a coaching change may lead to a championship in one season. As a coach, one must be able to give enormous value to the students, but one must do so by connecting effectively so that the students perceive that the information has great value. The more the student sees value, the more they will apply it. The more they apply it, the more success they will get. The more success they get, the more they value coaching.

To be an effective coach, we have found that a coach MUST have the ability to do five things: Question, Understand, Structure, Tell Stories, and Trigger Passion. We will go through these in more detail in this chapter, but first we must understand in more detail the roles of a coach.

Roles of the Coach

Experience and Relevance

A coach is there to hold your hand if you need it. He or she is someone who has the experience and who has accomplished something that you too want to accomplish. For example, if you wanted to speak in front of a large crowd, would you go to someone who read a lot about speaking and watches speakers on television but has never actually spoken in public before? Or someone who has emceed events, won speaking awards, done many keynote speeches and knows the tricks of the trade having done so many? Logically, you would seek the one with practical experience who is preparing for another presentation themselves as you ask them.

Risk Assessment

With a coach, you can bounce ideas back and forth. At the same time, the coach is able to assess from his or her personal experience if that idea is good, bad, or ugly. Coaches will have experiences to share so that you can understand why an idea will work or not. Numerous times, we have been approached by students asking us if the speech they have prepared is impactful, what questions should they ask to get the audience engaged, or if they should stand at a certain spot while at a certain part of their speech. We are always able to give sound advice for them to assess themselves. Whether they decide to act upon the advice is up to them but, at the very least, they now have something to consider.

Personally, from our business stand point, we do not do anything relating to our business unless we consult with our own coaches. Why run the risk of doing something wrong and suffer the consequences, when you have an expert who can answer questions? Questions like *"What will happen if we do this?"*, or *"What if we try that?"* Coaches are able to take your situation and assess it with multiple scenarios so that you can clearly identify the pros and cons of each decision and what to expect after you have made the decision. Imagine yourself driving a car along the side of a mountain. It curves and turns unexpectedly. Would you go slowly or fast? Would you be scared or confident? What if you had someone sitting beside you who drives that path every single day? Someone who is able to tell you when the next turn is, where it gets narrow and where it drops. Would you not be more confident driving that path? Would your chance of succeeding be greater? Is your risk managed?

MAKE MORE WORK LESS by CONNECTING

Foresight

Being able to guide you and show you where you can go is an important trait of a coach. For example, imagine if you wanted to climb mountains but were too scared and unsure how to do so. You seek a mountain climbing coach who is able to train you and prepare you for your very first climb. The first mountain may be short but to you, it is a great feat. It takes time with your mindset, confidence, and training for your coach to show you that you too can climb that "short" mountain. One day, you conquered all doubts that you have and you have successfully reached the top of that first short mountain that your coach has set for you. Now that you are at the top, your coach says, *"Now let's prepare for that one and I'll show you how."* And they point to the taller mountain across the river. You look up and up and think, *"Wow. That is crazy."* But, in fact, that is exactly what you said about the first mountain that you just finished! After months of training, mind setting and hard work, you make it to the taller mountain. You stand there proud as ever and your coach says, *"Now let's attack that one, an even taller one."* You see, a coach is able to show you where else you can go, how far you can grow.

Working with our students/clients, we show them how to acquire their first rental property or prepare for their first speech, then their second and third all while showing them the other possibilities that they have to *Make More* and *Work Less*. To a coach, these are things they have already done, but to you it is something you may have never thought to do.

We are often asked, *"Are people able to invest or do what they want to do without a coach?"* The answer is *"Yes"* they can. However, it will take more time, research, risk, and hard work to do so. A coach is there to speed up the process and get you to where you want to be faster with more success and less risk and growing pains.

Continuous Growth

As we have mentioned before, a coach's foresight is truly your greatest asset. He or she is able to help you to grow continuously to become more than you may have thought. It all comes down to what your goals are. If you plan on just buying your first home or doing one speech and don't want to do any more afterwards, then great, you will need only a coach for that first time and you may not need to have continuous coaching. However, if you would like to build a business and accumulate more properties and speaking engagements and truly *Make More* and *Work Less*, then continuous coaching is something we highly recommend. Many look at coaching and see it as an expense. That is the mentality that is preventing them from reaching higher goals. For instance, if you wanted your child to become a great piano player who will become famous one day, would you hire an 18-year-old who just finished their teaching exams because he or she was inexpensive? Or would you hire a pianist who has been performing for 20 years? Which piano coach will get your child to success sooner? Which coach will save more time? If a coach is able to net you thousands of dollars by giving you a tip on how to structure your presentation to impact more customers, was their fee not worth it then? If the coach is able to help you negotiate a better deal on the property and saves you $20,000, is their fee not worth it?

Top Five Things to Master

After understanding the roles of a coach, we can now see how: Questions, Understanding, Structure, Storytelling, and Passion enhances the coach's ability to connect with the student/client leading to greater successes.

<u>Questions</u>

Asking the right questions at the right time is the very first step to becoming an effective coach. By doing so you will gain the knowledge that you need to know your student/client or know your audience.

"Quality questions create a quality life. Successful people ask better questions, and as a result, they get better answers." – Anthony "Tony" Robbins

The better the question, the better the answers. The better the answers, the better a coach is able to assess how to add value.

Asking questions is like shining a flashlight toward the unknown. When the light is pointed in the right spots, what was hidden is now found. For instance, let's look at the following conversation:

Student: "I don't like speaking in front of people."

Coach: "What part of speaking in front of people do you not like?"

Student: "I don't know. I just don't like it."

MAKE MORE WORK LESS by CONNECTING

Coach: "Is it because you don't know what you are going to talk about?"

Student: "No. I know my information inside out."

Coach: "hmm. Is it because you get nervous when people are looking at you?"

Student: "No. I can sing and dance on stage without any problems."

Coach "Oh OK. What do you think is different between you performing and you speaking in front of people?"

Student: "I don't know. It's just different."

Coach: "Tell me how you feel when you are performing?"

Student: "I feel free, confident and able to express myself."

Coach: "Interesting, and how do you feel when you are speaking in front of people?"

Student: "I feel confined and trapped. Very rigid for some reason."

Coach: "I see. When you speak in front of people is there usually a podium?"

Student: "Yes"

MAKE MORE WORK LESS by CONNECTING

>Coach: "Have you ever given a speech without a podium?"
>
>Student: "No, not a formal speech, but after performing, I usually say a few words to the audience."
>
>Coach: "And how does that feel?"
>
>Student: "It feels great, just like when I perform."
>
>Coach: "Have you tried doing a formal speech without the podium? It sounds like the podium is confining you to act a certain way or to present information a certain way. Once you see a podium you feel that you must use it and stand behind it. Speak and move a certain way. And because of the podium being in front of you, hiding you from the audience, you feel confined and trapped. Next time you speak in front of people, try standing in front of the podium and see how you feel."

Notice how the questions led to more information? How it guides the issue down a path toward a solution? The quality of questions will allow you to develop a quality connection with the student. It shows the student that you care and want to add value. When the questions are effective, more trust is built.

Understanding

The more questions you ask, the more understanding you have for the student. As you understand your students' more, you will be able to either reflect back to your experiences or imagine what it is like from their perspective. Being in their shoes will allow you to come up with better ways of

MAKE MORE WORK LESS by CONNECTING

connecting with your students. So much so that you are able to say the right things at the right time.

When we were writing our first book, our greatest struggle was the battle between our ears – our mindset. We kept asking ourselves: *"Who are we to write a book?"*, *"What right do we have to write a book when there are so many books out there talking about the same thing AND written by people who are more famous than us?"*, or *"That person over there knows so much more about financial options, why would they read our book?"* On and on we went convincing ourselves that we are not worthy of becoming authors. Our coach, who had helped many others write their first books, who himself was an author, had gone through this many times, understood that our issue was worrying about things that we could not control, it was a confidence issue and a perspective issue. By simply saying three things, it changed our outlook completely:

1) *"Over the last 100 years nothing new has been written, only written in different voices. Your voice has not been heard."*

2) *"If people do not read your book, then they are not your target audience. Focus on those who are your target audience and let them hear your voice."*

3) *"Think back to when you started this path, would you find what you know now worth reading?"*

Those words struck us so effectively that writing our first book became the easiest part of having the book completed. Not only did those statements help us grow our series of books, but it also applied to us when we encountered our first

MAKE MORE WORK LESS by CONNECTING

speaking engagement, our first coaching client, our first real estate project, etc. It gave us foresight and continuous growth as new challenges come.

It is because a coach understands the students that the coach is able to realize what the potential is for the students. The results of challenging continuous growth is unlocking a student's potential.

<u>*Structure*</u>

With all that information, references, and knowledge, a coach must have some structure. To be effective, a coach's thoughts must be organized in a way for the student to understand what the coach is asking of them or presenting to them. For instance, while we coach speakers, we ask questions to find out what their purpose is. If the purpose is to inspire and motivate their audiences, to contribute more to their communities or donate more funds, then we can suggest what stories to use and how to present the stories. After suggesting the techniques and skills to implement into their speech, we will then explain why, by presenting it that way, it would have greater impact on the audience. Either through explanations, examples or role playing, the reasoning must be understood. A template, format or structure is in place for the information to be delivered to the student. We would not instantly suggest that he or she should wave their arms a certain way or to tell stories of no relevance if we did not first find out the purpose and later explain to them why. If structure is not in place, the student would be confused, and connection is lost.

As explained earlier in this book, methods like: T-T-T and Funnel In and Funnel Out, have their uses for certain

MAKE MORE WORK LESS by CONNECTING

purposes as does a speech done chronologically. Likewise, as a coach, how and when we present information, questions and techniques to a student must be done in a way that resonates most effectively for that student.

As a coach, with the questions and understanding, we must also realize that everyone is unique and has his or her own styles. There is a fine line between challenges and the impossible. The last thing a coach wants to do is to challenge a student to do something that is:

1) Impossible at the time, or
2) Takes away the character and personality of who the student is.

Challenges are to be given in such a way that allows the student to grasp its possibility. It may still scare them a little but not so much that it drives them away. Therefore, presenting challenges for continuous growth must be done with some structure. Think back to the story of climbing mountains. The coach challenges the student with a small mountain first, then a bigger one, then an even bigger one. While presenting the first challenge, the coach would show how it is possible. The coach would not have presented the biggest mountain first. That would be without any structure and be considered impossible by the student at the time.

The coach needs to present the possibilities of the challenge while also maintaining who the student is, how far is too far for the student. Are the tasks helping the student grow to become a stronger individual? Does that take away certain traits that are good and true to who the person is? Or does it enhance the student with another skill set. For instance. If a student truly loves talking about environmental topics, a

MAKE MORE WORK LESS by CONNECTING

coach's role is to show how they can effectively talk about those topics by enhancing the student's body language and vocal variety. What the coach should not do is convince the student to change topics if the coach isn't interested in the topic. Likewise, if the challenge is for the student to face the fear of public speaking, instead of having them do a three-hour talk right off the bat, have them do a five-minute talk about themselves and ease them into something they did not think they could do. As the saying goes: *"All in Good Time"*, having proper structure is critical in connecting effectively for a coach.

<u>Storytelling</u>

The most effective way for a coach to connect with their students is in storytelling. Through storytelling the student can relate to the story and possibly see themselves in the same situation. If the story tells a tale of overcoming adversity and challenges, then the student can apply the lessons to themselves if they have the same challenges. In most cases as coaches, we generally find students relate to personal stories. The following is one that we use while illustrating the power of mind set:

> *"We have all heard of the saying, 'Whether you think you can and whether you think you can't, you are right'. It is astonishing how what we think will determine the results of what we do. If I asked you right now to NOT think about Batman riding on Superman while singing 'I can show you the world...' what are you thinking about? Exactly what I asked you NOT to think about. Just picturing something you do not want happening actually causes you to make it more likely a possibility. So instead of thinking "I will*

MAKE MORE WORK LESS by CONNECTING

NOT screw up my talk", think "I will do awesome! My talk will be Great!". If you keep thinking the negative you will start psyching yourself out. Many years ago, when I performed a song on stage, this very thing happened to me. I practiced and practiced. I knew the lyrics. I knew exactly when to start and what to do. However, no matter how well I knew my routine, I couldn't shake the fear of forgetting the lyrics. Throughout the night, right up to the moment I was about to go on stage, I kept reminding myself NOT to forget the lyrics. Don't Forget! DO NOT FORGET! I recited the lyrics over and over again so that I will NOT forget. And just then, 30 seconds before I went onstage during my last run through in my mind of the lyrics. I stumbled. I panicked, and I stumbled again. Now I'm really psyched out! I went on stage thinking "don't screw up!" and started singing. When the part where I stumbled before I went on stage came, I blanked. My mind was empty and I stood there awkwardly as the music continued playing. At that moment I realized that because I kept thinking about NOT messing up, I forced myself to actually mess up, just to prove that I'm right. And therefore, as Nido says: 'Garbage in is NOT garbage out. It stays and gets pregnant!"

By telling that story, students see that as coaches we too have gone through challenges and adversity, and that we too are able to overcome them. Stories allow us as coaches to connect with the student. Our stories about how we got to where we are today, how we bought our first investment property, or how we prepared for our first speech competition, allows us to relate and connect to the students and teach through our experiences.

MAKE MORE WORK LESS by CONNECTING

Coaches who are great storytellers will also be able to draw from stories of others when the story fits. Some students after getting to know us need more than just our references and points of view, and therefore, our stories and experiences are not enough. In those cases, we will use stories of our friends, other students/clients and other successful individuals to get our message across. For instance, here is a story on how powerful your mind is.

> "Sometimes, it takes the success of others to show you that something that you thought was impossible is actually possible. Once you see that it is indeed possible, you start thinking that it is possible for you as well. Prior to 1954, running a mile in four minutes was impossible. Nobody believed it could be done and sure enough, no one did. It was not until Roger Bannister completed a mile in four minutes, that all of a sudden, so many others were able to beat what used to be an unsurmountable time. It was Roger Bannister that proved to people that it was possible and, in turn, others started to believe they could do it too.
>
> If you want to be a comedian and have had many difficulties succeeding, look at Jerry Seinfeld. He was booed and jeered off the stage during his first stand-up routine. He went home and believed that he could do it. He went back to the same stage and did the same routine and this time succeeded. He later moved on to do a show about nothing – Seinfeld, is now considered a class act and a legend among his peers. How are you different than who he was before he was famous?"

MAKE MORE WORK LESS by CONNECTING

Reaching for the right stories at the right time (structure) enables the coach to connect effectively with the student. More importantly, stories last longer. The student will draw on those lessons over and over again as we all still do today.

<u>Passion</u>

Finally, PASSION! As a coach we must have the passion to teach others, the passion to inspire and the passion to help others unlock their potential. When a coach is passionate in what he or she does, he or she is full of energy, full of excitement and full of inspiration. That fullness comes out with emotional storytelling, great body gestures and effective vocal variety. The coach will be able to come up with the right questions, understand better and have more effective suggestions. That energy and passion will then be absorbed by the student. The student will feed off that excitement and follow suit, giving the coach more attention, more energy, and more trust. Just imagine how you feel when you are at a sporting event, and they are announcing the players that scored the home team's goal versus that of the visiting team.

"SCORED by number 99! WAYNE GRETZZZZZZZKYYYYY. Assisted by number 17! Jari KURRRRIIIII!"

VS

"scored by number 14 Theoren Fleury"

Think about the worst class you have attended. Chances are great that the professor did not even look like he or she wanted to be there. Hence you keep falling asleep in that class. Whereas something as complicated as computer coding can be so exciting when explained by someone like

MAKE MORE WORK LESS by CONNECTING

Steve Wozniak (co-founder of Apple) who absolutely LOVES the topic.

There have been many occasions where we would be coaching a speaking student where we would take what he or she has presented to us and present it back to them with passion, energy, and emotion. After experiencing his or her own story through our presentation, he or she would apply it and feel the difference that allows them to impact and connect with the audience better. As coaches, we must let our students feel the passion that we have. By doing so a stronger connection is made and results will come.

Results, Results, and Results

After realizing that, as coaches, we had to ask quality questions, understand, have structure, become better storytellers, and have passion in what we do, we found greater results in our students. Students became more engaged with what we had to say, they absorbed the information with trust, and their energy levels escalated.

During our first effective speaking workshop to a group of young adults, we realized that purely teaching the skills and techniques of effective communication was not getting through to them. The students did not seem engaged. They did not seem like they were having fun and some could not wait for the class to be done. Instantly, we adjusted our teaching method to include more activities, more group discussions and asked more questions. On top of all that, we also increased our level of energy and engagement. Although we shortened the length of time that content was to be presented, we presented with higher energy, more effective body language and emotion. By teaching with

MAKE MORE WORK LESS by CONNECTING

activities, the students were much more engaged and paid more attention during the lecture portions as well. Due to the increased engagement, we found that elements of our lectures were evident in their speeches and presentations. Shortly after we were receiving praises from parents as to what a great job we did with the students and also students thanking us for teaching them so much and how we helped them become more effective speakers and stronger leaders. That feeling of impacting and inspiring a younger generation is like no other feeling.

After a while, we begin to realize that asking quality questions, understanding your audience better, having structure, telling stories better, and having passion, brings results in all aspect of our lives. By asking effective questions, we were able to find quality tenants. It is because we understand our partners better, that we are able to have joint venture projects that meets everyone's needs. With effective structure, we are able to organize events that are engaging and entertaining. It is because our storytelling skills are improved, that we are able network with more people and connect with more individuals. And finally, because we find the passion in what we do, we are able to emcee and host events with energy, excitement, and engagement. As more and more positive results come, the more you will value the power of effective communication and connecting.

Be a Coach

As we grew with the skills from being coached, we quickly realized that there was another level of learning the skills of effective communication, and that was to become a coach ourselves. When you coach others, you will find your own style and methods of effectiveness. You will carve your own

MAKE MORE WORK LESS by CONNECTING

way of asking questions and understanding. You will find your stories to tell and the structure of presenting information. Ultimately, as you coach and the results come, you will find your passion grows. And as your passion grows you will become an even more effective coach. The Circle of Coaching. Therefore, if there was one thing, we would encourage you to do, to enhance your communication skills and your ability to connect with others, would be to coach others. The rewards are endless.

As a bonus gift to our readers, we would like to offer you a free download copy of our book: *Make More Work Less: The Guide to Unlocking Your Potential to Live and Work on Your Own Terms*. Whether it is to invest yourself or have someone do it for you, there are many strategies that can be used to set you up to *Make More* and *Work Less*.

Please go to www.makemoreworklessbook.com/team.

MAKE MORE WORK LESS by CONNECTING

MAKE MORE WORK LESS by CONNECTING

Chapter 11 – Coaching Connects

"Words and pictures can work together to communicate more powerfully than either alone."

- William Alberta Allard -

Assurance Keys to Connecting

- Coaching is a concept that is tried, tested and true.

- Always Add Value

- Roles of a Coach
    o Experience/Relevance
    o Risk Management
    o Foresight
    o Continuous Growth

- Five Elements of Coaching
    o Ask Quality Questions
    o Understand your Audience
    o Organize and Structure
    o Storytelling
    o Passion

- Results, Results, Results

- Be a Coach

MAKE MORE WORK LESS by CONNECTING

Chapter - 12 -
Connect Through Stories

MAKE MORE WORK LESS by CONNECTING

MAKE MORE WORK LESS by CONNECTING

The Power of Storytelling

How did you learn not to talk to strangers? How about the importance of believing in yourself? Could it have been from stories like *Little Red Riding Hood*? *Star Wars*? Disney movies like *Hercules* and *Mulan*? The fact is great messages are delivered through great stories. They make the point more memorable, more relatable, and much more engaging for the audience. Notice how many of the examples throughout this book were given in a story form? The example of AT&T, the story of driving in other countries, or the story of the goalkeepers and penalty kickers. Once we mentioned those stories, you instantly remember them and their messages. Looking at the examples given by our fellow experts: Gloria Bosma, Dr. Ganz Ferrance, Chan Kawaguchi, Shin Kawaguchi, Stacy Richter, and Glenda Sheard, it was evident that they also utilized the power of storytelling to explain themselves and transmit their message. All successful individuals have great storytelling skills.

Steve Jobs, Walt Disney, Winston Churchill, Martin Luther King Jr., Oprah Winfrey, and Howard Schultz, use the skills of storytelling masterfully to encourage, inspire, and motivate all while entertaining their audiences.

> The 1984 Apple Macintosh commercial shows Jobs' ability to adopt from other sources (in this case, George Orwell's novel), apply it to his brand of Apple and tell a story so effectively that it changed the perception of computers to what we know today. Jobs flexed his storytelling muscles again though *Toy Story* when he was a part of Pixar.

MAKE MORE WORK LESS by CONNECTING

Winston Churchill and Martin Luther King Jr. inspired thousands upon thousands of people with speeches that are filled with powerful words such as:

> *"You ask, what is our policy? I can say, it is to wage war by sea, land and air with all our might and with all the strength that God can give us; to wage war against a monstrous tyranny never surpassed in the dark, lamentable catalogue of human crime. That is our policy."* – Winston Churchill

> *"We have also come to this hallowed spot to remind America of the fierce urgency of Now. This is no time to engage in the luxury of cooling off or to take the tranquilizing drug of gradualism. Now is the time to make real the promises of democracy."* – Martin Luther King Jr.

These speeches were put together will such skill and craft of a storyteller that it is no surprise that they are some of the greatest influential people of history.

Starbucks stems from the story of Starbucks Chief Executive Officer Howard Schultz's childhood. Schultz, who was seven years old at the time, remembers the accident vividly.

> *"That image of my father, slumped on the family couch, his leg in a cast unable to work or earn money, and ground down by the world is still burned into my mind,"* said Schultz.

They had no health insurance, no worker's compensation, no severance, and no way to make ends meet. Schultz vowed that if he was ever in the position to take care of people, he

MAKE MORE WORK LESS by CONNECTING

would strive to make a difference in their lives. His story later became the foundation of Starbucks under Schultz' leadership: Health benefits for part time workers, tuition assistance and employee stock purchase programs, etc.

"Starbucks has become a living legacy of my Dad", said Schultz.

As he tells this story to aspiring entrepreneurs, he has motivated a whole generation of young business men and women to change the world, help others and create their own economy.

The great Oprah Winfrey displays her skill in her movies, her poetry, her television show, her magazine, and in her replies in interviews. The following is an excerpt of her thoughts on the importance of storytelling. Her reply feels like a story:

> *"If my sense of storytelling began anywhere, it was in my grandmother's dining room. There I learned to love the sound of language and how words hold a cadence. There I learned to listen, to know when a story was about to take a turn, when the ending played out slowly, like grosgrain ribbon let loose from a package, or suddenly, like a door slamming in a gust of wind. The women in my grandmother's house kept up their spirits with stories of love and grief, anger, and laughter. They did not mince words, but they did drag out the truth in a string of metaphors and parables. What is a story but a way to help us see, if only for a second, the ways of the world in a new light?"*

For storytellers, Walt Disney would be second to none. His ability to relate and understand his audience was displayed

MAKE MORE WORK LESS by CONNECTING

in his feature films and shorts. Not only did he tell stories in his films such as *"The New Spirit"* as mentioned earlier in this book, but he also made sure that all the rides in his amusement park Disneyland told a story. It is because all the rides tell an individual story that the rides are no longer rides but an adventure, an attraction for guests to experience again and again. Long waits seem faster as you go through a story during the wait, and the experience lasts longer as the story gives it an emotional connection.

As you can see being a great storyteller will allow you to encourage, motivate, and inspire others with effectiveness. Combined with all the skills and techniques explained in this book, you will be able to connect with ease and *Make More Work Less.*

Learn From Everywhere

When the storytelling is effective, something can be learned from anywhere. Ever wonder why you enjoy a certain television program or a certain speaker? It is probably because they were able to frame the information with great storytelling. One can always gain insight when he or she asks "WHY?" The more you ask why you like or dislike something, the more you will be able to alter and tweak your own style, adding what you like from others and removing or improving elements of your style that you found you did not like from seeing others do it.

For instance, the television series *The Flash* is a very successful series. By asking why *The Flash* is so successful and why its storytelling is so effective, we soon found out that there is a rule that each episode of *The Flash* must have:

MAKE MORE WORK LESS by CONNECTING

Humour, Heroics, and Heart.

If any episode is missing any of the three elements, that episode is not completed and will not be approved. Does each episode have an emotional element? Does each episode get you sitting at the edge of your seat? Do you laugh in each episode? If you said yes to each of these, you probably enjoy the show.

So how does this apply to us as storytellers? Well, to be an effective communicator, a speaker who connects with others, you may consider having those same three elements in your talks. When you tell stories have stories that: bring excitement, stories that have an emotional pull, and stories that bring comic relief to the audience. By doing so, you will retain your audience for a longer period of time, as you will not be providing endless stories with humour or stories with just excitement. The most effective stories are those that support your message while at the same time provide Heroics, Humour, and Heart.

For those of you who are fans of this genre, you will notice something else that the series *The Flash* does very well in its storytelling, and that is the willingness to refer to other characters and pop culture. There would be crossovers from other television series, such as *Arrow* and *Supergirl*, and pop culture references such as *Star Wars* or *Back to the Future*. This shows that writers of *The Flash* understand their audience very well while at the same time relating to those who aren't pure *Flash* fans. This is no different than what the storytellers at *Marvel Studios* are doing with *Captain America*, *Iron Man*, *Black Panther*, and *Guardians of the Galaxy*. They are creating a universe that allows them to tell a story from many different points of view, reaching out to

MAKE MORE WORK LESS by CONNECTING

more people and connecting with people of all ages, cultures and preferences.

Outside the entertainment industry, we can find examples of storytelling everywhere. Commercials for Coca Cola tells short stories expressing the tagline of *"Open Happiness"*. When we go to a job interview, we are basically telling the interviewer a story about our past. Wouldn't it be most advantageous for you if you were the most memorable interviewee there? Wouldn't you want to be someone who not only connected well with the answers but also someone who gave so much that you have left the interviewer wanting more? So much more that the company hires you?

From a charity point of view, we are always given stories of the lives you changed when you donated. Those who have the most captivating story will most likely be able to raise the most funds. For relationship coaching, business consulting, and mentoring, we learn best because they have been though the experiences and are able to guide us toward the right direction. As you can see storytelling is the most effective way to get messages across to others, pass information and to teach. In fact, storytelling has been the oldest form of education known to humanity. The better the stories are, the more they are passed from generation to generation. Whether by cave sketches, written or spoken words, stories are what made each of us who we are today.

Think Quick on your Feet

A lot of our day-to-day lives consist of thinking quick on our feet. Many believe that effective public speaking happens when we are in front of an audience with a well thought out speech. However, that is only one aspect of effective public

MAKE MORE WORK LESS by CONNECTING

speaking. Other types of public speaking involve impromptu speaking. When asked to do impromptu speaking, many believe that they are weak at it. When one asks a few questions, all of a sudden, the person who says he or she isn't effective speakers, become instant speakers in public.

On many occasions, during coaching in our effective speaking courses, we come across students who struggled with their first speech in front of their peers. They would walk up to the podium, nervous, and scared. Constantly looking down, saying "Ahs" and "Ums", and could not wait to get back to their seats, all while saying that they have nothing interesting to say. Watching them stand in front of their peers is a very courageous act of willpower, they are facing their fears and jumping from their comfort zone. Once we ask them questions like:

- What is your favorite thing to do and why?
- Who inspires you the most and why?
- Where do you want to travel to the most and why?
- What do you think your strongest traits are and why?
- What are your greatest accomplishments? How did you feel? Tell us about the experience.

Without hesitation, most of the students are able to answer the questions, and continue talking way past the required time without nervousness, without stumbling and with eye contact. Something that we noticed when the students answered these questions was that many would do it in the form of a life story or stories that they got from elsewhere. This illustrates that we are all capable to being formal speakers and impromptu speakers. Once we add structure as we discussed in Chapter 4, emotions as discussed in Chapter 3, and understanding of who we are talking to as shown in Chapter 2, we can become effective communicators and connect with effective impromptu speaking.

We recommend that everyone should have several stories on hand that they can use in any scenario. Stories about something you learned, something that surprised you, something that inspired you and something that changed your world, can be used in multiple scenarios. Whether these stories are your own or those that you got from reading or talking to other people, stories are a great strategy to connect with your audience and also prepare you for impromptu situations.

Keys to Storytelling

Similar to the structure for developing an effective speech, having a structure for effective storytelling is also very important. There are eight main elements of a story: the purpose, the setup, pattern, foreshadowing, characters, relatability, the twist, and the passion.

Purpose – Why are you telling this story? How does this story add value to your listeners? Is it for entertainment? Is there a message? Did someone say something that reminded you of the story?

> *Example: Purpose – To show that action cures fear.*

Setup – This is background information that is needed for the story to have an effect on the listener. The setup should be short and have information that is important to the delivery of the story. You don't need all details if the details are not relevant to the story itself.

MAKE MORE WORK LESS by CONNECTING

> *Example: Setup – For our wedding, we decided to have the ceremony and celebrate it with our loved ones in Orlando Florida.*

<u>Pattern</u> – Something that is the regular norm for the situation. This is most likely something that will be changed as the story progresses.

> *Example: Pattern – A family member of ours has never been on a roller coaster.*

<u>Foreshadowing</u> – This is related to the pattern. A statement that indicates something will happen against the pattern which most can predict.

> *Example: Foreshadowing – Prior to the trip, we have been warned by this family member that there is no way they will go on any roller coasters.*

<u>Characters</u> – All stories have characters, you may be one of them. In fact, stories where you are involved have a greater impact. If the listener does not know the characters well, it is good to give a brief description of the character's personalities.

> *Example: Characters – This aunt of mine was always afraid of heights and high speeds, and I being the caring nephew was going to screen all the rides first before letting my aunt know that the ride is OK for her to ride.*

<u>Relatability</u> – Your listener has to relate to something in the story. Interest is only there if the listener can pull from past experiences what your story is about to say.

MAKE MORE WORK LESS by CONNECTING

Example: Relatability – Who here has been on the rides at Universal Studios? Who here has been on the ride - The Mummy? Great! So, you know how that ride goes. Well, who here has had moments where their memory fails them? Well, my memory did a number on me. Throughout the entire trip, I was able to remember the rides that were good for my aunt and the ones that were not until I got to The Mummy Ride. During the line, all I remembered about the ride is that it was a nice slow ride that goes though the scenes of the film. Constantly, I reassured my aunt that it was OK and that there was nothing to fear. And then, IT happened. The lights turned off, and instantly, I remembered this part of the ride. At full speed, we went backwards, forwards, quick turns here and diving turns there, a full-fledged roller coaster. I looked over to my aunt and there she was grasping at her chest, eyes shut tight and screaming at the top of her lungs! After the ride, I felt horrible. I quickly went to her to see if she was all right. She glared at me and gave me the disappointed index finger waving point.

<u>Twist</u> – This is the punch line, the part of the story that gives the full impact. The "Ah Ha" moment of your story that supports the telling of the story.

Example: After that ride, I was extra alert as to which rides were OK or not. I did not want to go through that again! We came across the ride Expedition Everest, a roller coaster at Disney's Animal Kingdom. Great attraction. Instantly, I told my aunt NOT to go on the ride. To my surprise, she said "Why not? I'll go because everyone else is." Not only did she go on that ride, but she also went on all the other rides on the trip

MAKE MORE WORK LESS by CONNECTING

AND enjoyed them. It has become an accomplishment that she is proud to tell her brothers and sisters, who do not go on roller coasters, how she enjoyed it. If that does not prove that ACTION CURES FEAR, I do not know what would.

<u>Passion</u> – As we have discussed in Chapter 4, passion is a very important element in speaking and more importantly in storytelling. The more passion you have in your storytelling the more your vocal variety, body gestures, and your emotions will come. That is what great storytellers do. Great storytellers are passionate people who are effective communicators and speakers who connect with their audience and individuals.

Stand Up and Laugh

As we have mentioned, one can learn from anywhere and anyone. For effective communication and storytelling, some of the most obvious places to learn from are attending live seminars, going to events with professional, motivational speakers or watching videos online (great resources can be found in the back of this book). Another great and absolutely amusing way to learn great storytelling and effective communication is watching comedians and illusionists. Stand-up comedy encompasses all elements of great storytelling and effective communication. It is an honest form of entertainment with instant feedback. If the comedian does not connect with the audience, the audience will not laugh and, in turn, the comedian will need to adjust his or her delivery, his or her material and his or her pacing. The comedian will do what he or she can, to get the audience back on his or her side. Watch as comedians pause and give the punch line in the end. Witness how they set up their stories. Observe how they engage the audience with their bodies, their actions, and their vocal variety. Listen to how they adjust on the fly, tapping into their impromptu speaking skills. Ultimately, absorb how they tell their stories, how they structure their talk and how they use the audience's emotions to get the laughs. For illusionists, they have to misdirect the audiences or their tricks won't work. Therefore, they tell stories to keep audiences from paying attention to the hands or elements in the tricks. Paying attention to how they structure their stories to keep audiences away from the trick will help you perfect your storytelling.

By studying great comedians and illusionists like Jerry Seinfeld, Chris Rock, Russell Peters, David Copperfield, and Penn Jillette and Teller, do their routines and monologues, one can find that there is a lot happening on stage and that one can learn and adapt for their own speeches or presentations.

Preparation and Practice

As with everything in life, nothing happens overnight. We must gain the confidence in ourselves and go through the steps of confidence as discussed in Chapter 1. To become an effective communicator and connect with ease, we must prepare and practice the art. Join organizations like Toastmasters, Dale Carnegie, or find a coach, as we mentioned. Put yourself in situations where you need to deliver speeches, network, or emcee events. Force yourself to grow your skills. With every opportunity you get, record yourself, review your own presentations and ask for feedback from others. While asking others for feedback, have them focus on the following items, and while you are evaluating yourself, use the same questions:

MAKE MORE WORK LESS by CONNECTING

- What did you see?
- What did you hear?
- What did you feel?
- What did you enjoy most?
- What suggestions do you have for me to improve on?
- Did you have fun?
- Were you engaged?
- Did you get the message?

If it is your first speech then write out the speech and practice it again and again until it flows naturally. Later, use cue cards or have the outlines prepared as you perfect your storytelling skills. Hiring a coach or joining speaking workshops may also be an option for you if you wanted to hone your skills and master public speaking and networking. The more time you put into learning, growing, and practicing the more you will be able to connect effectively.

**Nine-P Phrase to
Help Remember the Importance of Practice:**

MAKE MORE WORK LESS by CONNECTING

Prior Proper Preparation Prevents Poor Performance Of the Person Putting on the Presentation!

MAKE MORE WORK LESS by CONNECTING

Connecting with Effective Communication

By now, you are able to differentiate between communicating verses connecting. What effective communication means and how important connecting is. We hope you have been able to, through our stories and examples, witness how important finding the desire, knowing your audience and triggering emotions are to connecting with your listeners and audience. With the added skills of structure, body language, and vocal variety, it is easy to see how you can create powerful and effective speeches and interactions. By enhancing your abilities to tell stories, you are now able to deal with unexpected conversations, while, at the same time, allowing yourself to be more memorable and have your message get across to others most effectively. Finally, above all those aspects, you have realized that when you speak with passion, people listen and people will respond. With the stories shared by Gloria Bosma, Dr. Ganz Ferrance, Chan Kawaguchi, Shin Kawaguchi, Stacy Richter, and Glenda Sheard, it is obvious to see that effective communication is important in all industries and all areas of our lives. By releasing the power of effective communication and connecting, you will save time and effort, allowing you to *Make More and Work Less.*

MAKE MORE WORK LESS by CONNECTING

MAKE MORE WORK LESS by CONNECTING

Chapter 12 – Connect Through Stories

"Of all of our inventions for mass communication, pictures still speak the most universally understood language."

- Walt Disney -

Assurance Keys to Connecting

- Storytelling is the oldest form of learning.

- Stories encourage, motivate, and inspire.

- Heroics, Humour and Heart.

- All successful individuals are great storytellers.

- Having well-crafted stories at hand allows for fast thinking on your feet.

- Eight elements of storytelling:
    o Purpose
    o Setup
    o Pattern
    o Foreshadowing
    o Characters
    o Relatability
    o Twist
    o Passion

- Learn from others like comedians and entertainers.

- Practice and prepare – the Nine Ps
    o Prior Proper Preparation Prevents Poor Performance Of the Person Putting on the Presentation

MAKE MORE WORK LESS by CONNECTING

MAKE MORE WORK LESS by CONNECTING

Public Speaking Tips

AUDIENCE is the most important aspect of public speaking. You are the messenger or the deliverer of information. When preparing and delivering a speech, we need to keep in mind that we are speaking to an audience.

BELIEVE in yourself! **BELIEVE** in your topic! **BELIEVE** in your audience!

CONCENTRATE on your message and the audience. This will help with any anxiety or nervousness you may be feeling.

Talk directly to the audience as if you are having a **CONVERSATION** with every person in your audience, one person at a time.

BREATHING will help you relax. Practice slow breathing.

Be sure to make **EYE CONTACT** with members of your audience.

FOCUS on your audience and the success of your presentation.

People will pay more attention to being entertained than being educated. Appropriate **HUMOUR** in a speech loosens up the audience and invites them to listen.

Ensure your topic is well-researched. If you are including statistics, ensure that the stats are correct and always include the resource of your information. Remember to, **KNOW YOUR MATERIAL**

MAKE MORE WORK LESS by CONNECTING

OBSERVE the reaction of your audience.

PAUSES replaces filler words like ahs, ums, ands, buts, so...

PREPARE, PREPARE, PREPARE! "By Failing to Prepare, You are Preparing to Fail" – Benjamin Franklin

PRACTICE your speech standing. If you need to use notes, use index cards for the key points of your speech.

QUOTES are a great opening or closing tools for your speech.

Check out your **SMILE** in the mirror. See what your audience sees.

Ensure your **SPEECH** is organized with:
1. **Opening** – Have a strong opening statement or questions.
2. **Body** – Have three points to support your topic (depending on length/type of speech or presentation).
3. **Conclusion/Closing** – End your presentation with a strong message like a call to action, a famous quote, a positive statement, or a rhetorical question.

Use **STORIES** and anecdotes to illustrate and reinforce the main points of your presentation. Stories are easier to remember, and they make your presentation unique.

Always have a glass or bottle of **WATER** available for when you are speaking.

LISTEN and SILENT are spelled with the same letters. An effective communicator listens as well or even better than he or she speaks.

- FINAL THOUGHTS -

Thank you for taking the time to read our book. We have put a lot of effort into making it as straightforward and easily understood as a guideline on how to *Make More and Work Less by Connecting*. We felt that by adding practical tips, we could give you the keys to the problems you could encounter.

By now, you have already learned about the following:

1) Mindset
2) Connecting versus Communicating
3) Strategies, techniques, and skills for effective speaking and storytelling

You might be thinking, "I read your book, what's next?" Well, that's a valid question. We've found all too often that a book, while comprehensive, sometimes leaves us with some questions we want answered. To help you move even further along, we have compiled a collection of videos from the best authorities in the market to help you. The members of our power team and our coaches have answered the most commonly asked questions in their fields to add value for our treasured readers.

For more information on this, please visit www.yourarea.ca. If you have any questions you wish to have answered regarding this book, please feel free to e-mail us at makemoreworklessquestion@yourarea.ca. Please note that we get plenty of questions and e-mails daily, but we will do our best to answer your questions.

MAKE MORE WORK LESS by CONNECTING

We will now leave you with one last quote from Dr. Phil. "Anyone can do something when they WANT to do it. Really successful people do things when they don't want to do it." So, go out there and reach your dreams!

About Gloria Bosma

Gloria Bosma is a passionate educator, award-winning speaker, and relentless advocate for the Trisomy 18 community. Her highly energetic, wildly creative, and extremely compassionate teaching style have earned her APEGGA Teacher Award recognition, and many hugs from students, colleagues, and parents. Gloria infuses her speaking engagements with this same enthusiasm. She is a keynote presenter, workshop facilitator, and emcee. Her dynamic interactive workshops on "Cultivating Creativity" allow audience members to experience an equal dose of side-splitting laughter, fully engaged participation, and fabulous ideas to bring to their work or personal life. Gloria also touches lives and brings hope to those who have travelled the road of adversity as she shares from the depth of her soul the anguish of shattered dreams to the hope that is available to each of us.

MAKE MORE WORK LESS by CONNECTING

When she is not teaching or presenting, Gloria enjoys acreage living with her husband, son, and four-legged friend, Bandit.

Gloria Bosma
Email: gkbosma@gmail.com

About Dr. Ganz Ferrance

I am an International speaker, author, and entrepreneur. I have a doctorate in counseling psychology and a master of arts in developmental psychology from Andrews University in Michigan.

I'm also the former public education director and vice president of the Psychologists' Association of Alberta.

Since 1991, I've been helping individuals, couples, families and corporations reduce their levels of stress, improve their relationships, and enjoy more success.

I've been in the media a lot since 2003 having been interviewed by *The Edmonton Journal*, CBC Radio, 630 CHED, *Good Morning Canada*, CTV News, *Psychology Today*, *Ebony Magazine*, Bloomberg Business Radio Network, and many other media outlets. I hold the John C. Patterson Media Award from the Psychologists' Association of Alberta and the Rosalina Smith Award from the National

MAKE MORE WORK LESS by CONNECTING

Black Coalition of Canada for Exceptional and Prolonged Service from an Individual from the Black Community Conducting a Business.

My deep belief in "positive psychology" helps YOU be the best version of yourself. My style is straightforward, down-to-earth and no-nonsense. I pride myself on being a fellow "work-in-progress" and I put my blood, sweat, and tears into everything I present. This approach has made ME a sought-after public speaker with audiences in the United States and Canada, enjoying my fun, engaging, and life-changing presentations on beating stress and building superior relationships. I also have a black belt in karate and am currently studying Aikido. I live in Edmonton, Alberta with my wife and two children.

For a FREE download of my book "The Me Factor" audio go to: https://askdrganz.com/pages/giveaway

Dr. Ganz Ferrance
Ganz Team
Mobile: 780-428-5433
Email: happiness@askdrganz.com
Website: askdrganz.com

MAKE MORE WORK LESS by CONNECTING

About Chan Kawaguchi

Chan Kawaguchi is a strong-willed entrepreneur with a fiery spirit. Chan's ability to take a personal interest in others, allows her to connect and befriend anyone she meets. Chan's passion is to serve others and help them grow. Being able to communicate at a deeper level and get to know others propelled her to become the top agent of her insurance company in Canada within the first six months after starting. This was with no sales background. Chan will admit to not being 'tech-savvy' but has built businesses in real estate, insurance, cryptocurrency, and her latest venture, online marketing. With all this success, her proudest accomplishment is raising two children and enjoying as much time with them as possible.

Chan Kawaguchi

MAKE MORE WORK LESS by CONNECTING

About Shin Kawaguchi

Shin Kawaguchi is an avid learner who loves to teach and share his knowledge. Shin has the desire to learn and improve, and looks at losses or poor outcomes as learning events. With a passion for learning, Shin has been involved in real estate as both an investor and agent, financial services, cryptocurrency, and online marketing. Coming from a technical background as an engineer, Shin enjoys building systems and coming up with new investment strategies. Being an investor, Shin knows that most investments and deals do not actually go as planned. Communicating with team members, investors, clients, and contractors is vital, especially when things are not going as planned. Shin's latest venture is learning online marketing and has created a YouTube channel to learn the process of monetizing and branding online.

Shin Kawaguchi

MAKE MORE WORK LESS by CONNECTING

About Stacy Richter

Stacy is better known as the Marketing Mindbender. To kick-start his career, Stacy completed his bachelor of commerce degree at the University of Calgary with a double major in marketing and information systems. This was quickly followed by completing an industrial marketing minor at the University of Kaiserslautern in Germany.

He has successfully led marketing initiatives in nearly every sector known in the business world including oil and gas, e-commerce, retail, hospitality, manufacturing, professional services, finance, and fintech.

What you might not know about Stacy is that

- o He was once a winner of a beauty contest in Monopoly.
- o Stacy enjoys playing guitar and the harmonica but not at the same time.
- o He performed a song he wrote and produced on the *Buck Shot Show* when he was five years old.

MAKE MORE WORK LESS by CONNECTING

Stacy completed his MBA at the University of Phoenix before joining a boutique marketing agency as a senior associate. At the time of his exit four years later, he and the partners had grown the agency to six offices and 30+ associates across North America.

He has since been pursuing his venture career through acquiring and growing small to medium sized businesses. Stacy lives his philosophy of *Ask Great Questions, Get Great Answers* through his marketing agency PinPoint Strategies and the Marketing Mindbender platform. For bonuses, visit: https://www.marketingmindbender.com/make-more-work-less-bonuses

Stacy Richter
Email: stacy@stacyrichter.com
Mobile: 403-875-2772
Website: www.stacyrichter.com
Facebook: www.facebook.com/TheRealStacyRichter/
Instagram: www.instagram.com/therealstacyrichter/
Linkedin: www.linkedin.com/in/therealstacyrichter/
Twitter: twitter.com/therealstacyr

About Glenda Sheard

Glenda brings a dynamic, motivational and captivating manner to her speaking engagements, always mixed with a dash of humour. Glenda has a unique way of engaging and inspiring others. She provides customized presentations and workshops, encompassing a positive and unique connection with her audiences.

As a speaker for A Compassionate Tomorrow, Glenda Sheard brings heartfelt compassion to the floor from her life experiences – From Broken to Blessed – impressing upon her audiences the importance of gratitude and appreciation, and encouraging successful outcomes in enhanced self-esteem. With her experiences as a keynote speaker, special events emcee, and host of numerous workshops, Glenda also draws on her experience in media relations as well as her role as a fundraising professional and community volunteer. Glenda strives to ensure her speaking engagements are designed to be both enlightening and captivating.

MAKE MORE WORK LESS by CONNECTING

Glenda's Communicate with Confidence program teaches individuals and teams how to enhance their communication and leadership skills. Ultimately, enhanced communication and leadership skills boost self-confidence and empower individuals. Enhanced communication in the workplace will increase productivity and helps to boost team morale.

Glenda Sheard is regularly called upon as a speaker and emcee within her community. Whether she is moderating a political forum or emceeing a community event, Glenda utilizes her enhanced communication skills and focused motivation to better connect with her audience.

Glenda Sheard
Website: glendasheard.com
Blog: darrelsmom.wordpress.com
LinkedIn: Glenda Sheard
Twitter: @GlendaSheard

- For Additional Content -

Visit us at:

www.yourarea.ca
www.meetfongchua.com
www.makemoreworklessbook.com

Social Media:

Facebook: @FongChua
            @AssuranceRealEstateAcquisitionsInc
Youtube Channel: yourAREATV
Twitter: Fong Chua
LinkedIn: Fong Chua
Featured on Results Radio
Video Series: MakeMoreMindBites

Books:

Make More Work Less by Creating your Gateway to STARDOM:
Skillset Diversification, Tame Stress, Assess Risk, and DOMinate the Unknowns

Make More Work Less:
The Guide to Unlocking Your Potential to Live and Work on Your Own Terms

Make More Work Less with Cashflow:
The Step-by-Step Keys to Finding, Acquiring and Maintaining Cashflow Investment Properties

Make More Work Less by Building a Team:
The Secrets to Selecting, Building, and Maintaining an Ultimate Power Team

MAKE MORE WORK LESS by CONNECTING

All *Make More Work Less* books are available on Amazon or connect with Fong Chua at www.meetfongchua.com.

Recommended Resource List

MINDSET
Millionaire Underdog – JT Foxx
Mindset for Success – Reggie Batts
Change your Mind, Change your Results – Shawn Shewchuk
The Magic of Thinking Big – David Schwartz
Think and Grow Rich – Napoleon Hill

GOAL SETTING
Double Your Income Doing What You Love – Raymond Aaron

RELATIONSHIP BUILDING
How to Win Friends and Influence People – Dale Carnegie
Crucial Confrontations – Kerry Patterson, Joseph Grenny, Ron McMillan, Al Switzler
Crucial Conversations – Kerry Patterson, Joseph Grenny, Ron McMillan, Al Switzler

ONLINE RESOURCES

YouTube:

- From Success to Significance Dr. Nido Qubein Speaks for TransAmerica
    - https://www.youtube.com/watch?v=hDsZKtKZiDk&t=211s
- Nido Qubein: Leaders Go From Communicating to Connecting
    - https://www.youtube.com/watch?v=ZmrCTW-CyIU
- John Maxwell The Five Levels of Leadership
    - https://www.youtube.com/watch?v=aPwXeg8ThWI
- How to sound smart in your TEDx Talk | Will Stephen | TEDxNewYork
    - https://www.youtube.com/watch?v=8S0FDjFBj8o&t=2s

MAKE MORE WORK LESS by CONNECTING

- Body language, the power is in the palm of your hands | Allan Pease | TEDxMacquarieUniversity
    - https://www.youtube.com/watch?v=ZZZ7k8cMA-4&t=1s
- Think Fast, Talk Smart: Communication Techniques
    - htts://www.youtube.com/watch?v=HAnw168huqA&t=1762s
- The Art Of Effective Communication - Tony Robbins
    - https://www.youtube.com/watch?v=meLbMg7ySU4
- TedTalks

Websites:
- Nido Qubein – "How to be an Effective Communicator"
    - www.nidoqubein.com/
- John C. Maxwell – "Everyone Communicates, Few Connect"
    - www.johnmaxwell.com/
- Zig Ziglar – "Successful Persuasion through Public Speaking"
    - www.ziglar.com/
- Dale Carnegie – "The Quick and Easy Way to Effective Speaking"
    - www.dalecarnegie.com/
- Toastmasters Magazine
    - www.toastmasters.org/ToastmastersMagazine/ToastmasterArchive.aspx
- No fear Public Speaking
    - www.no-fear-public-speaking.com

www.ingramcontent.com/pod-product-compliance
Lightning Source LLC
Chambersburg PA
CBHW050442240426
43661CB00055B/2478